BLACK HAIR IN A WHITE WORLD

Black Hair in a White World

EDITED BY

TAMEKA N. ELLINGTON

The Kent State University Press ⬧ Kent, Ohio

© 2023 by The Kent State University Press, Kent, Ohio 44242
All rights reserved
ISBN 978-1-60635-456-8
Published in the United States of America

Cataloging information for this title is available at the Library of Congress.

27 26 25 24 23   5 4 3 2 1

To those who have been publicly shunned

and violated because of their Black hair

Contents

Part 3: The New Movement of Self-Acceptance of Black Hair

Foreword

Dr. Tameka Ellington is a Black hair griot. She is a keeper of stories, a rightful successor to the highest-ranked traditional storytellers of West African societies of the Fula, Hausa, Mandinka, Wolof, and Bambara. She is a venerable repository of oral tradition and a global advisor on Black hair. Through her scholarship and fashion exhibitions, Dr. Tameka has memorized and modernized the ancient intellectual investments toward hair for women of African descent. As a first-generation interdisciplinary scholar-activist, she has energetically merged wellness with fashion and Black beauty. She has communed with the archives of African ancestors to deify African aesthetic, resulting in a doctorate in curriculum and instruction and an associate professorship at Kent State University School of Fashion. She honors her griot predecessors by invoking fables and folklores to guide her readers and patrons through her award-winning healing work. While her peer-reviewed publications are prominently indexed when one enters the keywords *Black hair* into academic databases, she has graciously invited for hair scholars and practitioners to collaborate on an edited volume to navigate the Black hair phenomenon.

Critical stories about Black hair can disrupt the White world. The indoctrination of White standards of beauty idealizes long, straight hair and perpetuates the very existence of a race-based caste system. This indoctrination is chronic and ordered by systems of White supremacist racism that position White bodies and minds over all others. Considering the ramifications of self-esteem and self-efficacy for Black women, Dr. Tameka has invited contributions from members of the disciplines of sociology, psychology, fashion and retail, journalism and media, business, and hair care. The expansive documentation of the Black hair phenomenon through Black hair stories offers insight through the rigorous scientific study. Hair should no longer be weaponized for anti-Blackness but become an opportunity to agitate systems of oppression that denigrate the quality of life for Black women. Black hair stories deserve to be chronicled for students and professionals, novices and experts. *Black Hair in a White World* exemplifies critical stories about Black hair to drive social change.

The stories of Black hair began thousands of years ago. As documented through the papyrus and hieroglyphs of the Ancient Egyptian, or Kemetic, pyramid walls, Black hair was deemed sacred. Hair was a complex love language to the physical and spiritual world. It communicated family groupings, marital status, births, bereavement, and even needs for self-care.[1] Intentionally, European colonizers and plantation owners desacralized hair by misnaming Black hair *wool* or *fur,* to dehumanize people of African descent. For centuries during legalized chattel slavery in the Americas, Black Americans were denied the time required to reinvigorate the power of their hair and beauty rituals. Here, the stories of Black hair have become linked with trauma and misuse. Books like this can begin to decolonize Black hair stories and redirect centuries of grief into rebirth. This book reflects the intentional curation of all things Black hair.

What happens when someone understands your hair story? You feel seen. You feel heard. You feel cared for. As a clinical psychologist, hairstylist, and hair historian, I use hair as an entry point into mental health and wellness. I've dedicated twenty years to honing my skills in narrative therapy within Black communities, creating ornate hairstyles that make African tradition contemporary, and archiving the diverse lived experiences of hair. This has led me to become an expert on Black mental health and hair, testifying on hair discrimination in front of local and national legislators, podcasting with Michelle Obama's hairstylist and the braider of the natural hair anthem queen Solange, developing and implementing curriculum for hair care professionals on mental health first aid, and publishing a dozen articles on PsychoHairapy—the psychology of hair.

From a stance of using hair stories to heal, this book resolves dilemmas within Black culture and the Black hair care industry. First, its contents can heal interracial tensions related to hair policies. Whether elementary school principals, CEOs of Fortune 500 companies, or high-ranking US military officials, White people in positions of institutional power should be required to receive education regarding the inherent racial biases in straight hair grooming policies. This book not only defines *texturism*—bias toward straighter hair textures, a term Dr. Tameka coined—but also documents years of evidence to highlight its consequences at places of employment and sites of education. No longer should microaggressions and microinvalidations related to Black hair be tolerated. Members of the Black community can begin to recognize the internalized experiences of texturism and related systems. However, we are conditioned to enact biases within our families, friendship circles, and other relationships. This book can help Black hair experiences make sense.

Within the Black hair care industry, professionals can use this book to foster the arguments that their work is more than just "doing hair." Hair care has the ability to heal and reunite people on a cultural mission, because hair is a critical tool for ritual. In traditional African societies, only those initiated into priesthoods could touch the crowns of others. They would have to study for years and years to master the arts and healing modalities of hair. Today, this book can serve as an education tool for stylists with decades of experience and those just entering the field of holistic hair care. We should all strive for excellence in all we do, especially when holding the responsibility and destiny of a community.

This book is therapeutic to students and scholars who have tried to articulate significant research and propose questions that resolve problems in daily life but whose area of focus is viewed as "cutesy." As academics, we are tasked with securing our own spaces within higher education to contribute to the scientific literature and ensure that our names pop up like corn kernels from library databases for dissertating graduate students and those preparing to present at annual conferences paid for by professional development budgets. Institutions actively reject faculty applicants who do not align with the institution's branding. So, too, faculty members remove themselves from spaces that do not support their intellectual contributions or provide allowances for them to investigate their interests. And yet, Black hair is a subject rarely given space. We must ask, where do Black hair stories fit in research? This book offers creative studies into navigating Black hair and can serve as a point of expansion in garnering funds and refined instruments for research. The emotional labor of creating *Black Hair in a White World* must be commended. This tremendous task of eliciting the expertise of scholars and the burden of quantitative and qualitative rigor establishes *hair studies* as a reliable and valid entity. This book is not the end of the story but an opportunity to share more Black hair journeys.

AFIYA MBILISHAKA
Founder and CEO of PsychoHairapy,
Clinical Psychologist, Hairstylist, and
Hair Historian
Washington, DC
February 14, 2020

NOTE

1. Ayana D. Byrd and Lori L. Tharps, *Hair Story: The Roots of Black Hair in America,* 2nd. ed. (New York: St. Martin's, 2014).

Editor's Note

Tameka N. Ellington

Throughout this text, the term *Black* represents all peoples of the African Diaspora, while *African American* represents those of the diaspora who were born and raised in the United States. It is critical that when the term *Black* is used to describe a group of people, it must be used as a proper noun. In contrast, both *White* and *white* will be seen throughout the text. It was important for me, as the editor of this book, not to silence the contributors' voices. Everyone has their own rationale for capitalizing *White* or making it lowercased. In some chapters, *White* is capitalized for the same reasons *Black* is, as a means of expressing the humanness of both races of people. In other chapters, *white* expresses the stripping away of the white supremacist society that people of color are continually subjected to. Both choices are correct.

Throughout this volume, as well, sources cited that make use of broader ideas, approaches, concepts, or contexts, rather than simply providing specific quoted text, are referenced in full to draw readers' attention to the overall importance of these works.

Introduction

Tameka N. Ellington and Ladosha Wright

TAMEKA ELLINGTON'S STORY

As a Black woman, I have taken it as my mission for the last fifteen years to research Black beauty to understand why it is hated even after more than a century since Blacks were in bondage. I learned about the immense mental stronghold that the colonizing philosophies had on the world; Blacks and Whites have both been brainwashed to devalue the Black body. Along with other scholars, such as Ayana Byrd, Lori Tharps, Cheryl Thompson, and Ingrid Banks, I have been able to slowly chip away at the history of and negative connotations around Black hair—and the importance of redefining what Black hair is and can be.

When I was a young girl, I was told I had nappy hair and would be prettier with straight hair. My hair has been a source of trauma throughout my life. My mother took great pride in caring for my hair and my sister's; however, I was missing an element of beauty and femininity. I started noticing that the little boys always liked the girls with long, straight hair. These girls had all the friends, especially if they allowed friends to play with their hair. My fifth-grade year was one of my most challenging. I had the biggest crush on a boy in my class, and I remember always wanting to play on his team and be next to him in line as my classmates and I walked back into the school building from recess. One day as we shuffled in line to come back into the building from recess, I must have been overly enthralled by my crush, because he noticed! He laughed at me as he teased, "What you lookin' at, Napparoni?" Then, he belted out in song, "Napparoni, the San Francisco treat!"—lyrics he adapted from Rice-A-Roni's popular television commercial. I was mortified and heartbroken as the rest of my classmates stood there sneering and pointing. I was so hurt, but I laughed it off, to show that I was not phased. This was among the first of many traumas I would experience regarding my hair.

The summer of my first year of college, I decided to work for an amusement park, because I could live on its campus and maintain my newly found young-adult freedom. During the new employee orientation, management reviewed the policies and ground rules about living and working at the park. They mentioned the company uniforms and sneakers we would wear daily. Also covered were the rules restricting body adornments: no large tattoos, no piercings, and no wild hair colors. Further, employees could not wear Afros, braids, or locs—the natural hairstyles typically worn by Black people. I was taken aback by this policy, because I was wearing a cute, curly Afro. Management's final words were "Employees must look All-American." From that instant, I knew I would not endure an entire summer at that amusement park! After one month I returned home.

I could not deny the hunger for information about my hair. Why? Why can't I wear my hair the way I want? Why can companies dictate how Black people wear their hair? Is this right? How can it be? When I started my master of arts degree at Michigan State University, one professor told the class that we must begin thinking about our thesis topics. No other subject grabbed my interest the way Black hair did. Since then, I have been doing this work, and there is still so much to do.

Since 2002, I have published several academic articles and encyclopedia entries about Black hair. I am a designer and scholar, and much of my creative scholarship has been centered on Black art and culture. For many years, I dreamed of curating an exhibition with Black hair artifacts to tell the story of Black beauty. In partnership with African art historian Dr. Joseph Underwood, *TEXTURES: The history and art of Black hair* was born. The show opened in Fall 2021, featuring more than two hundred historical objects, artifacts, and contemporary works of art. The show encompassed a full story of Black hair, from ancient Egyptian artifacts to new works by artists such as Sonya Clark and Kehinde Wiley.

The phenomenon of Black hair continues to be a societal point of contention. Natural Black hair has been and still is criticized by non-Blacks and Blacks who believe the natural texture of Black hair is a problem. The devaluation of Black hair is a direct consequence of slavery. Slavery ended in 1865, and more than 150 years later, Black hair, still the brunt of jokes, is undesirable, heavily discriminated against, and overly manipulated to adhere to White beauty standards. This discrimination keeps children from going to school, prevents women and men from climbing the corporate ladder and insists that Black hair must acculturate if its wearer wants to be given half the chance at a happy, successful life. This is a global problem, and it is especially prevalent in the United States. A very few examples include the stories of Andrew Johnson, a wrestler who was forced to cut his hair during a match, Brittany Noble Jones, a news anchor who was fired from her job because she wore her hair in its natural state, and Faith Fennidy, a young girl who was asked to leave school because of her braided hair.

I am a former associate professor at the Kent State University Fashion School and interim assistant dean for the College of the Arts. My African-inspired exhibition and publications on the sociopsychological aspects of Black hair and dress are internationally awarded and recognized. Today, I am a motivational speaker working with schools and other institutions, training them on detecting and resolving issues of hair discrimination, as well as combatting low self-esteem caused by the dogma of Black beauty and hair.

CONTRIBUTING AUTHORS

As I was conceptualizing *Black Hair in a White World,* I began to dream of a text that would offer a diverse yet unified look at Black hair and culture. I have worked with and admired other amazing scholars focused on Black hair. Friends in academia from universities across the nation recommended that I consider working with their colleagues or newly graduated doctoral students. With the book, I wanted to be able to cover various aspects of Black hair, from politics to history and culture to Black hair movements of yesterday and today.

I am honored to be joined by such a talented, knowledgeable group of scholars and activists. Dr. Mikaila Brown is a trained anthropologist and a fashion designer. Dr. Lauren Cross is an interdisciplinary artist/filmmaker, curator, and scholar whose work has been screened and exhibited across the country. Dr. Annette Lynch is professor in the Textiles and Apparel Program at the University of Northern Iowa and the cofounder of the Center for Violence Prevention on her campus. Dr. Afiya Mbilishaka is a therapist, professor, research scientist, hair historian, and hairstylist. Dr. Talé Mitchell is assistant professor at the School of Media Arts and Design at James Madison University. Terresa Moses is a proud Black queer woman dedicated to the liberation of Black and brown people through art and design. Dr. Taura Taylor is a natural hair stylist in Atlanta, Georgia, and holds a BBA in finance from Howard University and an MA and a PhD in sociology from Georgia State University. Ladosha Wright has combined her career as an outreach worker and salon owner to style, write about, and advocate for Black hair.

Before the fifteenth century and the start of the transatlantic slave trade, the hair of Africans was glorified, decorated, molded, and braided. The adornment of hair dates to ancient Egyptian times. Hair was a significant component in the life of African people; it represented personal status among the Fulani, Himba, and Wodaabe tribes, to name a few. Hair was critical to African societies for the power it held.

History has revealed that slave traders consulted with notable European physician Johann Blumenbach and botanist-taxonomist Carlos Von Linnaeus, both of whom were known for their work in the classifying of humans. They chose positive and complimentary terms to describe the appearance and hair of Caucasian people. However, when describing African hair, they used descriptors associated with slaves, who were considered "half animal."[1] Four hundred years later, words like *woolen, kinky*, and *nappy* remain signifiers describing the textured hair of people considered the "lesser race."

Today, Black people's relationship with their hair has been shaped greatly by the transatlantic slave trade and colonization. According to Dr. Willie Morrow, barber, stylist, inventor, and author, "Freedom, dignity, and a sense of self-worth were lost when the comb was lost; for, without the comb, the hair was nothing, and when the hair is nothing, the individual becomes nothing as well."[2] *Black Hair in a White World* was also written as witness to the fact that hair discrimination still exists and needs to be rectified. The White standard of beauty will be discussed in depth in this text, and in some instances it will be referred to as White supremacy of beauty. The philosophy of White supremacy creates a societal structure that endorses and enforces the idea that all non-White forms of beauty are inferior and all people should strive to assimilate to the dominant, White model. As a result of this model, Blacks and Whites still have an adverse relationship with Black hair. This text aims to inspire its readers to love and accept *all* forms of hair and beauty.

In July 2019, in a step to deconstruct the idea that Black hair is inferior and unacceptable, California became the first state to enact a bill titled Creating a Respectable and Open World for Natural Hair (the CROWN Act) that prohibits discrimination against Black hair. The State of New York quickly followed with similar legislation aiming to treat those who wear their natural textured Black hair equally to their peers. Through loopholes, some are still being discriminated against. For instance, private schools are not required to follow the state-mandated dress codes that prohibit students from being singled out because of their hair. The story of eight-year-old New York City Catholic school student Jediah Batts, whose parents were told that he could not wear cornrows to school, is just one example.[3] Other states are also working toward their own bills to prevent Black hair discrimination. However, we still have a long way to go.

Intracultural racial discrimination continues to be an issue. In media and popular culture that caters to Black people, Black hair is still seen as ugly and/or a signifier of someone from a low socioeconomic status. In their music, artists such as Beyoncé, Nikki Minaj, Chris Brown, and Lil Wayne discuss their preference for "good." Unfortunately, the dogma of "good" (straight) hair and "bad" (kinky) hair, which started during the slave era, is still alive and well and perpetuates a message of self-hatred.

THE CONTEXT OF *BLACK HAIR IN A WHITE WORLD*

Black Hair in a White World was written to educate its readers about the complex and often controversial topic of Black hair. It will focus on perceptions of Black hair via popular culture and the media. Much of the substance of this text comes from analyzing books, films, advertisements, digital platforms, and other media. The lack of societal acceptance of natural Black hair will be discussed at length, along with the cultural uprising of Black people in the early 2000s, resulting in the need to educate themselves about their natural hair textures.

Critical social theory is a social philosophy developed out of Marxist theory in the late 1930s to challenge sociocultural understanding by offering a holistic critique of societal structure and a means by which to deconstruct it. Out of the 1960 Civil Rights Act, several other theories emerged that can be categorized under the critical social theory umbrella. Throughout the current text, various theoretical frameworks serve as lenses for understanding the phenomenon of Black hair and the difficulties that come along with forced assimilation and acculturation into a White supremacist standard of beauty. Molefi Kete Asante's Afrocentric theory, Patricia Hill Collins's Black feminist thought, Derrick Bell's critical race theory, Kimberlé Crenshaw's intersectionality theory, and Tsedale Melaku's systemic gendered racism theory, the main frameworks used in this text, all fall within the realm of critical social thought.

In organizing this text, I used Susan Kaiser's (1983) work "Toward a Contextual Social Psychology of Clothing: A Synthesis of Symbolic Interactionist and Cognitive Theoretical Perspectives."[4] Clothing, hair, and body adornment are elements of a larger field of study, apparel and textiles, which gives a comprehensive look at "dress," encompassing any type of human body manipulation. According to Kaiser, social interactions with clothing (in this case, hair) serve two functions: "(1) the negotiation of identities, and

(2) the definition of situations." These two-way interactions build culture and help to explain why people wear what they wear. The approach explains situations based on an individual's perception. Thus, our thoughts are often predetermined by societal culture.

Thus, this text is broken up into three parts. Part 1 is a look at media messages and the semiotics of the cultural history of Black hair. We start the conversation in chapter 1 with a historical evaluation of Black hair advertisements from the early 1900s through the early 2000s. This work is a comparative analysis of the messages from Black- and non-Black-owned hair care companies. In chapter 2, an analysis of Jacqueline Woodson's award-winning novel *brown girl dreaming* introduces the reader to the history of the Great Migration of Black people. Woodson discusses the metamorphosis of Black hair from the short-cropped hair of boys and the straightened, beribboned hair of girls in the South to the defiant Afros that became very popular in the north during the civil rights era.

Part 2 covers critical race theory and the sociocognitive approach to making meaning of culture. Chapter 3 gives an overview of pop culture and media influences on little Black girls' perceptions of their hair. Media targeted at Black girls has immense power over the ideology of Black hair. Thus, understanding these messages helps to control girls' cultural perceptions by giving parents the opportunity to intervene. Chapter 4 discusses the discriminatory perceptions of Black hair in the workplace, specifically Black hair styled in locs. This chapter starts with a brief history of the negative connotations associated with locs and how the stigma is prevalent today. Chapter 5 gives a phenomenological approach to understanding the quality-of-life shift Black women have after transitioning from chemically straightening their hair to wearing their natural texture.

Part 3 employs black feminist thought, providing a true understanding of the hair experiences of Black women. This part of the book discusses the symbolic interactions of the natural hair movement, a subculture of Black women who became one another's main source of support on their journey to wearing and loving their natural hair when the rest of the world was still unaccepting. The text explains what the movement is, how it started, and how it has evolved. Chapter 6 gives a comparative look at the 1960s Black Power and Black is Beautiful movements and their relationship to the natural hair movement of today. Chapter 7 is comprehensive work developed from the author's dissertation on the collective consciousness of Black men and women regarding their role in the natural hair movement. In an attempt to reframe societal beauty standards, this chapter discusses the deconstruction of anti-Blackness. Chapter 8 evaluates the technology involved in formulating the natural hair movement today. The author analyzes YouTube, Twitter, and other social media platforms that connect Black people. The final chapter of the book, chapter 9, walks the reader through an interactive symposium and exhibition called *Project Naptural*. This weeklong event included educational programming, hair styling demonstrations, community art, and critical conversations about deconstructing White standards of beauty to begin to create a safe place where patrons can start on a journey to self-acceptance.

This text is real, not sugar-coated in the least. It gives a true picture of the Black community's distress and how we have done all that we can to move past the hurt of slavery and colonialism. If you have ever had a question about Black hair and the realization that is Black beauty, you will find the answers to many of these here. In our current society—with the recent deaths of George Floyd, the many others that were slain before him, and those who continue to be slain after him—now more than ever, the necessity for a deeper community understanding is critical. You cannot fear what you know, and racial discrimination is an intermingling of fear and misconception of an entire race of people. So that our society can move forward, we must come together and develop a greater appreciation for each other. When you read this text, that is *exactly* what you will get: an appreciation for the cultural phenomenon that is Black hair—the struggle and the beauty.

NOTES

1. Raj Bhopal, "The Beautiful Skull and Blumenbach's Errors: The Birth of the Scientific Concept of Race," *British Medical Journal* 335, no. 7633 (2007): 1308–9.
2. Willie Morrow, *400 Years Without a Comb: The Untold Story* (San Diego: Black Publishers of San Diego, 1973), #19.
3. Michael Elsen-Rooney, "NYC Catholic Schools Hold Fast on Boys' Braid Bans Despite Laws Banning Hair Discrimination," *New York Daily News*, Dec. 2, 2019.
4. Susan Kaiser, "Toward a Contextual Social Psychology of Clothing: A Synthesis of Symbolic Interactionist and Cognitive Theoretical Perspectives," *Clothing and Textiles Research Journal* 2, no. 1 (1983): 1–9.

PART 1

Messages and Semiotics in the Cultural History of Black Hair

CHAPTER 1

Black Hair in Print Advertisements

A HISTORICAL ANALYSIS

Tameka N. Ellington and Talé A. Mitchell

Today, African American hair is a multimillion-dollar industry monopolized by non–African Americans. In the 1900s, ingredients including axle grease and ground animal bone marrow were used to make hair products in African American homes. Advancements in chemistry allowed wealthy entrepreneurs such as Annie Malone and Madame C. J. Walker to mass-produce hair and beauty lines; others outside of the African American community took notice of the financial opportunities and started businesses that produced and distributed African American hair care items.[1]

FIG. 1. The American Health and Beauty Aids Institute logo for 100 percent Black-owned hair care companies.

Producing and distributing African American hair products was such a lucrative business that non–African American communities with great access to ingredients and strong financial support began monopolizing the industry.[2] To combat this, the American Health and Beauty Aids Institute (AHBAI) was founded in 1981 to connect the African American community with quality hair products produced by African American–owned companies. AHBAI's marketing icon, the Proud Lady, symbolizes pride, hope, and dignity and promotes economic growth in the Black community (Fig. 1).[3] In 1986, Irving Bottner, former resident and chief executive officer of Revlon's Professional Products Group, stated, "In the next couple of years, the Black-owned businesses will disappear. They'll all be sold to the White companies."[4] In

response, Civil Rights activist Jesse Jackson and the AHBAI advised other African Americans not to buy products from Revlon and other non–African American hair product companies. This boycott was difficult to enforce, though, because non–African American brands tended to copy the products and packaging of African American products.[5] In 2004, the Black-Owned Beauty Supply Association was established to continue strengthening the presence and identity of African American–owned hair care companies.

The commercial hair products were created not just to manage and care for the hair but to aid African Americans in simulating and conforming to the dominant culture's beauty ideals. Hair-straightening products and bleaching creams became a means for survival and a signifier of freedom and progress.[6] After slavery was abolished, African Americans could not be employed if they were not "well groomed." Being appropriately groomed meant they had to straighten their hair and lighten their skin tone.[7] This beauty standard has been enforced since the late 1800s, especially in the media. Unfortunately, in many instances, it remains today.

This study evaluates the semiotics of decades of African American hair advertisements to indicate how those messages evolve over time. Research suggests that semiotics has been a popular means by which to study media because it helps formulate "a clear idea of what to look at when analyzing the meaning of media messages [and] explains why the media have differential effects; [which] enables the observer to analyze the structure of media messages without ignoring the interpretive processes of the audience."[8]

Media and mass communications researchers Dana Mastro and Bradley S. Greenberg found that African Americans were portrayed more negatively on television than Latinos and Whites.[9] According to Green, media sectors aiming products at the African American community must understand their only success at attracting African Americans is creating a strong ethnic identification displaying them positively.[10] Research shows that media companies owned by non–African Americans often portray African Americans stereotypically.[11] Specifically, African American women are often shown with overly sexualized personas.[12] News articles and images directly reflect the values and interests of the advertisers, usually White men.[13] These stereotypes are rooted in the dehumanization of African Americans during the slave era, when men, women, and children were treated like animals instead of human beings. Oversexualized, hypermasculine, lazy, and deviant images still plague the media today.[14] The African American ethnic identity is often portrayed incorrectly or negatively and bears little resemblance to the community's reality.[15]

Colorism, a term coined by Alice Walker, is discrimination based on skin color and results in the preferential treatment of light-skinned African Americans.[16] Colorism also involves the negative valuation of kinky textured hair, which researchers term *texturism*. This is another concept that both African American and non–African American companies fall victim to. Colorism was fostered due to the preferential treatment by light skin-toned house slaves received over dark skin-toned field slaves. This ideology is so deeply rooted that it has manifested into intercultural discrimination within the African American community, described in the Black self-hatred theory.[17] Throughout history, African Americans were taught that they were "bad" and "inferior." This led to a detrimental internalization of a negative self-concept in African Americans. In the past and still today, African Americans shown positively in the media have usually been visually appealing to the dominant society, that is, they have light skin tones and straight hair. Research suggests that all hair care companies have histories of creating advertisements using models with straightened hair, a direct reflection of the mainstream, White beauty standard, and mass media in general also privileges the mainstream, White aesthetic.[18] Journalist Tiffany Onyejiaka discusses the harsh truth that "[Colorism] indicates that Hollywood still overwhelmingly believes that a Black woman must possess European features to be considered beautiful or valuable."[19]

In knowing this history and the research results of others, it was critical to learn whether the media represented messages of accurate cultural values, behaviors, beliefs, and traditions.[20] Thus, messages were reviewed for proper use of African American Vernacular English (AAVE), the dialect spoken among the majority of working-class, urban African Americans.[21] Another way to determine the level of ethnic identity was to see whether the messages used stereotypical innuendo. The authors used content analysis (research method for textual material) to evaluate the imagery and vernacular of sixty-one African American hair product advertisements.[22]

STUDY RESULTS

The aim of this research was to differentiate between the African American hair product advertisement messages given by African American– and non–African American–owned businesses from the 1900s through the 2000s.

When evaluating the research results, the authors found four main communication variables: publication ownership, ethnic identity based on text vernacular, ethnic identity based on the physical characteristics of the model(s), and the message's purpose. Was the message solely about selling a product? Did it include information about styling and maintenance education, self-love, and cultural pride? Was the message created to get customers to conform to societal standards of beauty? Was it about standing out from the crowd?

To better explain the results, the authors found it essential to provide context regarding various elements of the African American physical characteristics. These were important to evaluate because media and marketing history has shown a preference for African American models in line with the White standard of beauty.[23] Thus, skin tone (light, medium, or dark), facial features (African or European), hair texture (straight, naturally curly or biracial, or kinky), hairstyles (permed, Jheri curl, weave, or natural hair), and the models' clothing (conservative, elegant, or provocative) were assessed.[24] The evaluation of these variables will aid in the discovery of how societal structures evolved regarding the physical characteristics of African Americans in the media.

Skin tone and hair texture have been sources of both power and degradation for African Americans, particularly women. Historically, African Americans with lighter skin and straighter hair have been considered more beautiful, intelligent, and wealthy. These individuals fit within the dominant ideal of beauty and solely based on their skin and hair and are considered less aggressive and easier to get along with than their counterparts who have darker skin tones and kinkier hair.

Publication Ownership

Once the advertisements were selected, the company holdings for each product were analyzed. The data showed that, on average, African Americans owned 70 percent of the hair product companies and non–African Americans 18.3 percent. The race of the owners for the other 11.7 percent could not be determined, because this information was not in the public record. Although there were ups and downs, African Americans remained the top owners of hair product companies. In the 1900s–30s, African Americans owned 60 percent of the businesses. In the 1940s–50s, the United States was still recovering from the Great Depression, and African American communities were affected the most; they "suffered from an unemployment rate two to three times that of Whites."[25] As a result, business increased for non–African American–owned companies. However, it was not by happenstance that in the 1960s–70s, 90 percent of African American hair product businesses were owned by African Americans. This period was one of uprising for the community. The Black Panthers were the trendsetters in the newly accepted Black-self era.[26] They were the first to wear their hair in Afros, influencing others in the African American communities to join the "Black is Beautiful" movement. In the 1980s, however, companies like Revlon began monopolizing the industry, and African American ownership dropped to 60 percent.[27] In the 1990s, organizations such as AHBAI were on the front line, fighting alongside African American businesses to regain ownership of their hair product companies. The support resulted in 90 percent of the industry being owned by African Americans. In the 2000s, African Americans gain lost much of the hair product market. Many of the suppliers of hair products were, and remain, Korean. It has been said that Koreans have purposely kept African American owners out of the beauty supply industry by not distributing their products to African American–owned hair supply businesses.[28]

The findings showed that there are some discriminatory messages using images and/or vernacular in non–African American hair product advertisements. Analysis of ad copy revealed no innuendos or stereotypes in the non–African American hair company advertisements. However, 66 percent of advertisements for African American–owned companies possessed significant ethnic identity via the vernacular. Further supporting the hypothesis, the models in the advertisements for African American companies had darker skin tones and predominantly African American features (full noses and lips), while non–African American companies used lighter skin-toned models with European facial features (thinner noses and lips). Even with a more mainstream advertising message, non–African American companies effectively captured enough of their African American customers' ethnic identities to make it difficult to differentiate the African American–owned companies from the non–African American–owned ones. This successful strategy assisted in non–African American–owned businesses' monopolization of the industry and is an example of the need for Black endorsement of affirmative action, in which African Americans needed the power to reclaim ownership of the African American hair care industry.[29]

African American Vernacular English

It was determined that throughout the century under analysis, advertisements for African American companies were influenced by current events. After the abolishment of slavery, African Americans had to acculturate to mainstream beauty standards, straightening their hair and bleaching their skin. A 1910 advertisement from Garrett Morgan urged customers to "improve your appearance" and "declare war on bad hair." Madame C. J. Walker claimed that her customers could go from the "cabin to the mansion" if they used her hair-straightening products (Fig. 2). These findings suggest that the self-hating good hair versus bad hair concept was prevalent in the African American community as early as the 1900s. The only way to gain success was to get rid of "bad," kinky, African textured hair. From the 1900s to the late 1960s, advertisements encouraged readers to assimilate to White standards of beauty. One example is the non–African American–owned company Hair Strate (Fig. 3).

Advertisements in the 1960s–70s were aligned with the civil rights and Black Power movements and heavily used AAVE. African American hair companies' advertisements connected to their consumers with verbiage that promoted self-love and Black pride while using AAVE and contemporary slang. African American–owned companies, Afro Sheen and Royal Shield used African influences. Afro Sheen used the term *pamoja!* The Swahili word for *together*. Royal Shield (1972) promised a closer connection to African roots by stating, "Royal Shield naturals lead a fuller life" (Fig. 4). AAVE was strong in other advertisements; one featuring singer James Brown exclaimed, "Hey! With your bad self—use Mystery of Black and be as bad as me!" (Fig. 5). In the 1960s and still today, *bad* is a slang term meaning that a person is the best at what they do and who they are. Even Clairol (1970), the only non–African American–owned company during this era, used AAVE to connect with customers: "Clairol frees the 'fro." In AAVE, words are often shortened; for example, *'bout* for *about, gettin'* for *getting,* and *'fro* for *Afro.*

The 1990s advertisements for African Pride products used AAVE. Its slogan, "Keep your head up," was borrowed from a song title from Tupac Shakur, one of the most famous African American rap artists of that time. Paradoxically, the company name, African Pride, contradicts its products. This company sells hair-straightening products, which erase the natural texture of one's hair while promoting confidence and pride in one's African roots.

The 2000s offered a few softer examples of using AAVE in advertisements. Shea Moisture, owned by Liberian inventors, urges its customers to "be natural. be you!" Positioning their products as usable by all women,

TAMEKA N. ELLINGTON AND TALÉ A. MITCHELL

their advertisements feature African American and White women, stating, "beKinky, beCurly, beWavy, beStraight." This has been very controversial, resulting in many African Americans turning away from the brand.[30] Would the Black endorsement of affirmative action be relevant for an African-owned company that is considered a "sell-out?" Another advertisement from the 2000s uses AAVE to position itself: Miss Jessie's is selling "the best darn curl cremes period!" The data suggests that using AAVE in the advertisements was an appropriate tactic for connecting with the African American community, even if African Americans do not own the company.

Physical Characteristics

Skin Tone

There was overlap regarding skin characteristics, as some companies used two or three models in one advertisement. More than 90 percent of advertisements used African American models with true ethnic features, such as wide noses and full lips. They used medium-skin-toned models 42 percent of the time, dark-skin-toned models 34 percent of the time, and light-skin-toned models 24 percent of the time. Models with dark skin tones were used in every era except the 1940s–50s. In the 1900s–1930s, skin bleaching creams were introduced into the beauty industry, and by the next decade,

Royal Shield Advertisement from 1972 (Copyright © by *Ebony Magazine*. Reprinted with permission.)

FIG. 5. (*right*) Cannolene Company, Mystery Black Advertisement, 1969 (Copyright © by *Ebony Magazine*. Reprinted with permission.)

they were available to the masses. These creams had become a part of many women's daily beauty regimens; not surprisingly, the beauty standard was for light skin. In contrast, dark-skin-toned models were used 60 percent of the time during the 1960s–70s, when promoting Black Pride was prevalent.

Notably, dark-skin-toned models were used 77 percent of the time during the 1990s. These findings contradict previous research that has discussed society's preference for light-skinned African Americans.[31] Tiffany Onyejiaka has addressed how actresses with light skin tones are still the majority in movies and that African American women have been more scrutinized regarding skin tone than their male counterparts.[32] The current data suggests that the number of print media advertisements adhering to the light-skin White beauty standard has decreased, similarly to the findings of Vanessa Hazell and Juanne Clarke.[33] These authors discussed that the compulsive need for African Americans to adhere to White beauty standards has decreased from the beginning of enslavement to the mid-2000s, while the number of African Americans following Black beauty standards has increased. It became evident that the models' skin tones paralleled trends in African American ethnic identity; however, it is assumed that light-skinned African American models are still preferred in mainstream television programs and movies. By this same notion, in 2016, on the high fashion runway, *Vogue Italia* discussed how models of color do not sell products as White models do.[34]

Hair Texture

During the decades under study, permed, or relaxed, hair remained consistently the preferred hairstyle. As many of the products promoted were hair straighteners, it follows that 80 percent of the models had straight hair. Every non–African American advertisement except one had a model with straight, or permed, hair. Natural hairstyles came and went in the 1960s–70s, but as soon as the Black Panther Party fell in the early 1980s, African Americans were on to the overprocessed style of the Jheri curl. In that decade, every model had chemically straight hair or a Jheri curl. And moving into current trends, one prominent natural hair blogger has stated that the natural hair movement of the 2000s is probably on its way out because women believe their natural hair is not seen as sexy; to be attractive, they must have straight hair.[35]

In all the advertisements evaluated, 22 percent of models had kinky hair. The kinky Afro was trendy in the 1960s–70s, and 80 percent of models had natural Afros. The second-highest percentage of natural kinky hair portrayals shone in the 2000s, with 50 percent of the models. This finding is parallel with the beginning of the natural hair movement. However, in these advertisements showing models with natural hair, 30 percent also featured women with straight hair. The data suggests that companies are

Physical Characteristics of African American Models in Hair Advertisements

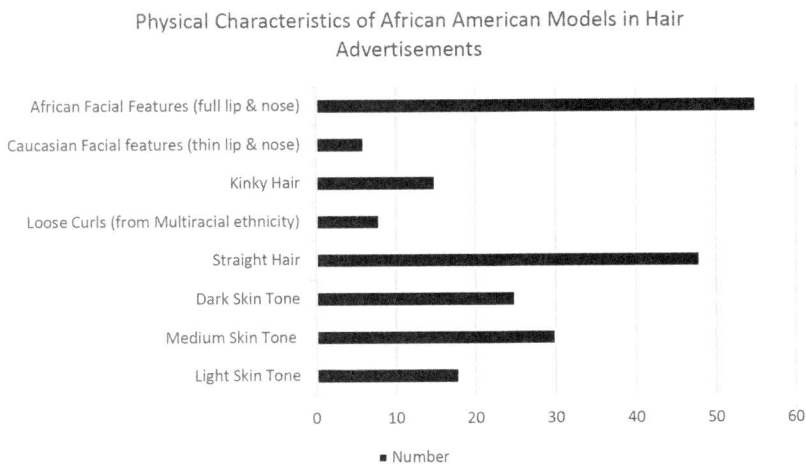

FIG. 6.
Physical characteristics of African American models in hair advertisements.

positioning themselves as providing products for women who wear natural hair and women who wear permed, straight hair. The data is divided by characteristics of the models: light, medium, or dark skin tones and straight, naturally loose curled (usually the result of multiracial ethnicity), or kinky hair. The authors also evaluated whether the models had European facial features, thin noses and lips, or African facial features, full noses and lips. (See Fig. 6.)

Hairstyles

The only hairstyle that remained consistent throughout the decades was straight permed or relaxed hair. In the 1950s, women wore hairpieces—either full wigs or wiglettes. In the late 1980s and early 1990s, celebrity African American women began wearing weaves.[36] Full head weaves were not adopted into the mainstream African American hair industry until the late 1990s and early 2000s. Today, weaves are a multimillion-dollar industry: according to industry leader Alix Moore, "More than 60% of women wear weaves."[37] In contrast to the weave is the natural hairstyle. The Black Panthers wore the first popularized naturals, Afros, in the 1960s–70s in correlation with the Black is Beautiful movement, which promoted self, cultural, and racial acceptance. Today's natural hair movement began in the late 1990s and early 2000s as an alternative to the weave. Its purpose was to return to self-love and accept one's kinky hair texture. Natural hair has often been controversial, and African American women who wear their hair's natural texture have faced discriminatory treatment and continue to do so. Natural hairstyles are sometimes considered "unprofessional" and even have caused some people to be fired from work or removed from school.[38]

Education

Selling the product was their main goal, although many advertisements served second and even third purposes. Of the sixty advertisements evaluated, twenty-one educated the consumer about the products. As former slaves found new freedom, hygiene and hair care became of the utmost importance. Acculturation into the dominant society was African Americans' mission,

FIG. 7. Garrett A. Morgan Hair Refining Company advertisement, 1900s.

and hair products were a major component of this. In the 1900s–1930s, hair products and the liberty to style one's hair as one wished were new; thus, advertisements had to be educational, and 70 percent of the advertisements of this era were: for example, see Garett Morgan's Hair Refiner Ad from the early 1900s (Fig. 7).

Another era when educational advertisements were prevalent was the 1980s, with 60 percent of advertisements having such a message. The new Jheri curl hairstyle was so different from previous styles that advertisement readers needed much information about the process, maintenance, and styling. The salon Jheri curl was so expensive that many of the hair advertisements showed potential customers the ease of doing the style at home with products such as Pro-Line's Curly Kit.

Conformity

As acculturation was the primary goal of African Americans in the 1900s–1930s, it follows that 70 percent of the period's advertisements relayed messages of conformity. Hair straighteners and skin bleaching creams were the two main beauty products on the market for African Americans. As time passed, African Americans built their own stronger cultural and racial identity; therefore, only 30 percent of companies in the 1940s–50s promoted acculturation. The societal dogma of acculturation was almost nonexistent by the 1960s–70s; pride in the culture became the main focus.

The data suggests that African American companies were more closely connected to the African American culture. The conformity message of the 1900s–1930s came from African American hair product companies, just as the 1960s–70s self-pride messages came from the African American hair product companies. After the abolishment of slavery, conformity and acculturation were the means of survival, because African Americans could not get jobs otherwise; thus, helping them conform was for the betterment of their community. Having self-pride in the 1960s–70s was again for the betterment of the community, and wearing natural hair was one way to show pride.

Clothing and Sexy Undertones

The clothing worn by the models in the advertisements was analyzed as conservative (everyday clothes with not a lot of skin showing), elegant (formal and evening wear), or provocative (tight-fitting clothes with skin showing). Some advertisements showed models wearing no clothing (headshot, including bare shoulders). In 11 percent of the advertisements, those featuring models with no clothes did not have a sexy or provocative undertone. Elegance was rarely the focus in the hair advertisements, with only 5 percent of the ads having formally dressed models. Models in 56 percent of the advertisements wore conservative, everyday dress. This finding does not

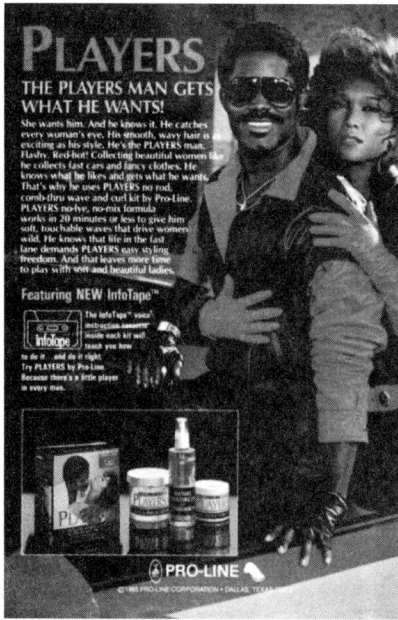

FIG. 8. Pro-Line (African American-owned company) advertisement from *Jet*, 1985.

support previous research, which states that African Americans are oversexualized in the media.[39] In the current study, 28 percent of the advertisements had sexy undertones. Therefore, through the decades, a substantial number of hair advertisements have been either conservative or sexy.

Like in other industries, sex sells in African American hair product advertisements. The advertisements of the 1980s and 2000s had the most sex appeal. Madonna and Cyndi Lauper were two of the most famous sexy, trendsetting performers of the 1980s. During that decade, 36 percent of the hair advertisement were very sexy and seductive. Both African American–owned companies and non–African American–owned companies were using sex to sell their products. Many advertisements displayed men and women in seductive poses and sexy clothing or none at all. These advertisements suggest that if the customer buys the product, their hair will be sexy, and they can win the girl or guy they desire. The African American company Pro-Line had a product called Players, with an advertisement that stated, "The Players man gets what he wants!" (Fig. 8).

Likewise, in the 2000s, 72 percent of the advertisements had models dressed in sexy clothing. In the 2000s popular culture, Paris Hilton and Kim Kardashian were two of the most influential socialites, both becoming famous after sex tape "leaks" (Hilton in 2004 and Kardashian in 2007). Out of the eight companies with sexy advertisements in the 2000s era, four were owned by non–African Americans and four by African Americans. All advertisements with sexy undertones promoted either permed or relaxed or weave hair products (Fig. 9). These findings suggest that society still buys into the ideology that you can only be attractive with straight and/or long hair. Again, these findings parallel the good hair versus bad hair phenomenon, which is a direct threat to the African America community.

CONCLUSION

The purpose of the current study was to compare hair advertisements for African American– and non–African American–owned companies since the start of the industry, in the 1900s. The data revealed no stereotypical innuendos in the advertisements from the non–African American owned companies. This is important, as it shows that even though the non–African American companies were not a part of the community, they knew enough about it to

FIG. 9. Mizani (non–African American–owned company) advertisement from *Essence* magazine, circa 2009.

promote their products with an adequate level of ethnic identity. However, the models in the advertisements from the non–African American–owned companies had light or medium skin tones and straight hair or weaves.

African American–owned hair product companies had a higher level of ethnic identity because they used models that physically reflected the majority of the population—medium skin tones with straight hair or weave. Only African American–owned companies promoted natural hair products. The cultural climate determined the physical characters of the models, the skin tone, and marketing copy used. For instance, in the 1940s–50s, African Americans had mastered acculturation into mainstream beauty standards. Bleaching creams, hot-comb pressing pomades, and hair-straightening creams were the biggest selling products. African American–owned companies used the zeitgeist to connect with the community. In the 1900s–1930s, African Americans were simply trying to survive after the abolishment of slavery; therefore, the messages were to assimilate into mainstream society for economic stability. The cultural climate of the 1960s–70s included Black Pride and no assimilation. African American companies used their products and advertisements to bring cultural awareness to their customers. For example, Royal Shields used imagery inspired by Zulu warriors. In the 1980s era of glitz, conspicuous consumption, and sex, both African American and non–African American companies promoted hair products with sexy advertisements.

Throughout all the researched eras, African American companies used AAVE to connect with their customers. Afro Sheen used the Swahili word *pamoja* to educate the community on its connection to Africa and to promote togetherness. Duke Natural, a 1970s company, said its product was "for men who wear it like it is." This phrase was a nod to the newfound cultural acceptance and ethnic identity. In contrast to the 1940s–50s, when men had straightened their hair with a lye-based concoction called a *conk*. Non–African American–owned companies used a softer version of AAVE. Thus, there appeared no differences between the advertisements for their products and those made by African American companies. This strategy helped non–African American–owned companies take control of much of the African American hair product industry.

From the 1900s to the 1950s, images were black-and-white photos and drawings, making it difficult to read the models' skin tones accurately. Copy in some advertisements was not legible, and the researchers had to give educated guesses about the tone and purpose of the messages. Even with thorough research, the ownership of five products could not be designated. The analysis for these advertisements was done the same way as all the others; however, these products could not be counted when comparing numbers between African and non–African American companies.

The current study contributes to further understanding African American media and culture. Future research may expand our knowledge of media catering to the African American hair industry by conducting a content analysis on television commercials. The data here shows that most models used in print advertisements to promote hair products had medium skin tone. It was hypothesized that television and films still expected African Americans to adhere to the standard of beauty; therefore, it would be important to evaluate how models are portrayed in televised hair product commercials. There is a foreseen challenge with this research: many African American–owned companies do not advertise their hair products on television. Typically, it is White-owned corporations, such as Pantene, that televise advertisements for African American hair products. Consequently, a thorough investigation will have to be done to find television commercials for African American–owned companies.

Through content analysis, future research may examine advertisements in the African American weave and wig industry. African American women wearing weaves has been a very controversial topic ever since the start of the full head weave. In the beginning, women were very secretive about whether they were wearing weaves, but today they are more open—hence, the line in Beyoncé's song "Get Me Bodied" states, "Pat your weave, ladies"; be proud of the weave you wear. Research has claimed that women who wear weaves or wigs have been accused by others of not being culturally conscious and not significantly identifying with their African heritage.[40] There is and has been an unspoken cultural divide between women who wear weaves (almost always coupled with permed hair) and those who wear their hair naturally. This phenomenon is yet another strain of the larger colorism intercultural divide. A better understanding of the weave industry and the natural hair industry is a step in the direction to minimizing the effects of the divide. Academic research cannot accomplish this alone; mass media is still responsible for the perceptions of African Americans. Until society as a whole becomes more culturally aware, respectful, and inclusive of all peoples, the struggle will persist.

NOTES

1. Ayana D. Byrd and Lori L. Tharps, *Hair Story: Untangling the Roots of Black Hair in America*, 2nd ed. (New York: St. Martin's, 2014).
2. "Blacks Meet with Revlon," *New York Times*, Nov. 14, 1986, accessed Dec. 19, 2017.
3. Elizabeth Johnson, *Resistance and Empowerment in Black Women's Hair Styling* (Burlington, VT: Ashgate, 2013), 48.
4. "Backstage," *Ebony*, Dec. 1986, 24.
5. "Blacks Meet with Revlon"; Johnson, *Resistance and Empowerment in Black Women's Hair Styling*; "Backstage," 25.
6. Joel Freeman, "Who Was One of Madame C. J. Walker's Most Important Role Models?," *Freeman Institute*, accessed Dec. 19, 2017, http://www.freemaninstitute.com/poro.htm.
7. Colorism is deeply rooted in slave-era mentality; enslaved people who had dark skin tones were field hands while those with light skin tones, often descendants of the master, were good enough to be housemaids, and, in some cases, even to educate. Media depicts models with light skin tones as the best and most attractive. Dark skin tone is a mark of oppression and behind much social suppression in the African American culture.
8. Francis Arackal, "Semiotics and Media," in *The Symbolic World: Construction and Deconstruction*, ed. S. Sekar Sebastian (Bangalore: Chapter Asian Trading Corporation, 2015), 1.
9. Dana E. Mastro and Bradley S. Greenberg, "The Portrayal of Racial Minorities on Prime-Time Television," *Journal of Broadcasting and Electronic Media* 44, no. 4 (2000): 690–703.
10. Corliss L. Green, "Ethnic Evaluations of Advertising: Interaction Effects of Strength of Ethnic Identification, Media Placement, and Degree of Racial Composition," *Journal of Advertising* 28, no. 1 (1999): 49–64.
11. Mastro and Greenberg, "The Portrayal of Racial Minorities on Prime Time Television."
12. Vanessa Hazell and Juanne Clarke, "Race and Gender in the Media: A Content Analysis of Advertisements in Two Mainstream Black Magazines," *Journal of Black Studies*, 39, no. 1 (2007): 5–21.
13. Yuki Fujioka, "Black Media Images as a Perceived Threat to African American Ethnic Identity: Coping Responses, Perceived Public Perception, and Attitudes towards Affirmative Action," *Journal of Broadcasting & Electronic Media* 49 (June 10, 2010): 450–67; Christy LaPierre, "Mass Media in the White Man's World," *Edge—Ethics of Development in a Global Environment*, June 4, 1999, Stanford Univ., https://web.stanford.edu/class/e297c/poverty_prejudice/mediarace/mass.htm.

14. Hazell and Clarke, "Race and Gender in the Media"; Mastro and Greenberg, "Portrayal of Racial Minorities on Prime Time Television."

15. Green, "Ethnic Evaluations of Advertising," 49–64.

16. Alice Walker, *In Search of Our Mothers' Gardens* (New York: Harcourt Brace Jovanovich, 1983).

17. Stephanie Irby Coard, Alfiee M. Breland, and Patricia Raskin, "Perceptions of and Preferences for Skin Color, Black Racial Identity, and Self-Esteem among African Americans," *Journal of Applied Social Psychology* 31, no. 11 (2001): 2256–74.

18. Johnson, *Resistance and Empowerment in Black Women's Hair Styling*, 2013.

19. Tiffany Onyejiaka, "Hollywood's Colorism Problem Can't Be Ignored Any Longer," *Teen Vogue*, Aug. 27, 2017, https://www.teenvogue.com/story/hollywoods-colorism-problem-cant-be-ignored.

20. Green, "Ethnic Evaluations of Advertising," 49–64; Alicia Fedelina Chávez and Florence Guido-DiBrito, "Racial and Ethnic Identity and Development," *New Directions for Adult and Continuing Education* 84 (1999): 40.

21. Walter F. Edwards, "African American Vernacular English: Phonology," in *The Americas and the Caribbean*, ed. Bernd Kortmann and Edgar W. Schneider (New York: De Gruyter Mouton, 2008), 181–91.

22. The number of advertisements ranged from nine to eleven for each of the six eras: 1900s–1930s, 1940s–50s, 1960s–70s, 1980s, 1990s, and 2000s. The selection criteria for the advertisements had three components; the media must first advertise a hair product, then show a frontal image of an African American person, and third, have at least one sentence or phrase. Earlier eras were combined (for instance, 1900s–1930s) because African Americans had little print media presence at that time. Consistent African American presence in mainstream media surfaced in the late 1960s, after the Civil Rights Act passed. The advertisements from the 1900s–1930s came from mostly newspapers.

   The *Pittsburgh Courier*, founded by Edwin Nathaniel Harleston in 1902, was one of the largest, most influential African American newspapers in the United States. The *Chicago Defender*, founded in 1905 by Robert S. Abbott, mostly focused on bringing discriminatory injustices to light. The *Chicago Defender* led the movement of the Great Migration when six million African Americans moved from the rural south to the North, Midwest, and West from 1916 to 1970.

   In May 1900, the *Colored American Magazine* became the first such periodical published by and for the African American community. Published until November 1909, it featured news, lifestyle articles, and beauty advertisements. In 1905, W. E. B. Du Bois founded the *Crisis*, the official publication of the National Association for the Advancement of Colored People (NAACP). The *Crisis*, an important magazine of the Harlem Renaissance, and the *Chicago Defender* are still in print today, now focusing on news, politics, and other current events.

   After the end of the Harlem Renaissance in the mid-1930s, African Americans continued to be excluded from mainstream media. This discrimination resulted in the creation of two of the United States' most popular Black publications: *Ebony*, founded in 1945, and its sister magazine, *Jet*, in 1951. *Essence* came along in 1968. Data collected from the 1940s–50s and beyond were taken from one of these three publications.

   Today, *Ebony* and *Essence* remain the leading publications catering to the African American community, each with a readership of over one million. *Ebony* was owned by the Johnson Publishing Company, an African American company; in 2016, the Clear View Group, another African American company, purchased the magazine. Essence Communication, an African American publishing company, owned *Essence* magazine for thirty-four years, until *Time*, a publisher, bought it in 2005. In 2018, *Essence* magazine again became a fully African American–owned publication when Sundial Brands purchased it.

23. Johnson, *Resistance and Empowerment in Black Women's Hair Styling*, 2013. Model's clothing—Conservative, elegant, or provocative: analyzing the clothing displayed in the advertisements was important because prior research found that African Americans were often over sexualized and are dressed more proactively than other races in media.

24. Hair texture can be straight, naturally curly, or kinky. The "good" (straight) hair and "bad" (kinky) hair divide, *texturism*, also results directly from colorism discrimination.

     The following terms are specific to African Americans' hair styling preferences or choices.

     - Permed or relaxed hair is natural curly or kinky hair that has been straightened by a creamy chemical product.
     - The Jheri curl is a permed hairstyle that was popular in the 1980s. The hair is loosely curled on rods and left with a glossy, wet look. It was named for its inventor, hairdresser Jheri Redding. This hairstyle came in a variety of curl patterns that differed from standard perms in the amount of moisture activator that was required to sustain the wet-look style. A Jheri curl damaged hair because the chemicals left it dehydrated.
     - A weave consists of synthetic or human hair extensions applied to the permed/relaxed or natural hair to add length and/or fullness. Weaves are usually applied by being either sewn to flat, braided hair for a longer lasting style or glued in for a more temporary style.
     - Natural hair—hair of those from African descent or peoples of the African Diaspora that has not been chemically straightened or altered, also known as virgin hair.

25. John Hardman, "The Great Depression and the New Deal Poverty and Prejudice: Social Security at the Crossroads," *Edge*, Stanford Univ., updated July 26, 1999, https://web.stanford.edu/class/e297c/poverty_prejudice/soc_sec/hgreat.htm.

26. "The Power of the Panthers," *CNN*, Feb. 16, 2016, http://www.cnn.com/2016/02/16/us/gallery/black-panthers/index.html.

27. Byrd and Tharps, *Hair Story*.

28. Emma Sapong, "Roots of Tension: Race, Hair, Competition and Black Beauty Stores," *MPR News*, Minnesota Public Radio, Apr. 25, 2017, https://www.mprnews.org/story/2017/04/25/black-beauty-shops-korean-suppliers-roots-of-tension-mn.

29. Byrd and Tharps, *Hair Story*.

30. Samantha Schmidt, "Shea Moisture Reaches Out to White Women in Hair Products Ad. Black Women Protest," *Washington Post*, Apr. 25, 2017.

31. Coard, Breland, and Raskin, "Perceptions of and Preferences."

32. Onyejiaka. "Hollywood's Colorism Problem Can't Be Ignored Any Longer."

33. Hazell and Clarke, "Race and Gender in the Media."

34. Valeria Maltoni, "Vogue Italia All Black Issue Goes Viral," *Conversation Agent*, accessed Oct. 28, 2022, https://www.conversationagent.com/2008/08/vogue-italia-black-goes-viral.html.

35. "The Natural Hair Movement Coming to an End? Creamy Crack Taking the

World Back?," *StrawBerriCurls*, Oct. 16, 2013, http://www.strawberricurls.com/natural-hair-movement-coming-end-creamy-crack-taking-world-back/.

36. Byrd and Tharps, *Hair Story*.

37. Alix Moore, *The Truth about the Human Hair Industry: Wake Up Black America!* (Palm Beach Gardens, FL: American Hair Factory, 2012), 38.

38. Tameka N. Ellington, "Social Networking Sites: A Support System for African-American Women Wearing Natural Hair," *International Journal of Fashion Design, Technology, and Education* 8, no. 1 (2015): 21–29; Cheryl Thompson, "Black Women, Beauty, and Hair as a Matter of Being," *Women's Studies* 38, no. 8 (2009): 831–56.

39. Hazell and Clarke, "Race and Gender in the Media," 5–21.

40. Thompson, "Black Women, Beauty, and Hair as a Matter of Being."

CHAPTER 2

Analyzing Jacqueline Woodson's *brown girl dreaming*

THE SEMIOTICS AND MEANING-MAKING OF BLACK HAIR

Annette Lynch and Tameka N. Ellington

Memoirs provide an authentic route into the lives of others that contain potential qualitative data that can be used to expose patterns of significance central to understanding and interpreting the importance of dress and appearance to the cultural construction of identity. This study evaluated Jacqueline Woodson's memoir *brown girl dreaming* to explore the management of Black girls' identity by self and female relatives.[1] The events of the book take place during the civil rights era South and the years following the Great Migration in the North.[2] This chapter will also explore the changing meanings associated with hairstyles as Woodson moves in space and time, from the South to the North and from the beginning of the civil rights movement to the Black Power movement.

brown girl dreaming is a National Book Award–winning verse novel for middle-grade and adolescent readers. Krystal Howard classifies Woodson's awarding-winning work as an example of confessional poetry and a problem-based verse novel, both linked to contemporary American poetry and children's literature.[3] Confessional poetry, which emerged as a literary form in the United States in the 1950s and 1960s, is associated with the poetry of Robert Lowell and his students Sylvia Plath and Anne Sexton, and John Berryman and his *Dream Songs.* Most often cited is Lowell's *Life Studies,* a highly personal story in verse form of his life and family relationships. That confessional poetry empowered previously hidden voices to use the art form to articulate and share traumatic private experiences and emotions.

Jacqueline Woodson uses the verse novel genre and confessional poetry with a different intent—to empower voices hidden by the endemic racism that served and continues to serve as an often invisible underlying structure to social and cultural life in the United States. Confessional poetry, with its focus on acts of self-positioning and self-definition, is ideally suited to give voice to Woodson as she uses her position as a writer to "put on the page . . . stories of people who looked like me."[4] In her childhood, she "was a child on a mission—to change the face of literature and erase stereotypes. Forever." In Woodson's own words:

> brown girl dreaming is the story of my family, moving from slavery through Reconstruction, Jim Crow, and the civil rights movement, and ends with me as a child of the 1970s. It is steeped in the history of not only my family but of America. As African-Americans, we were given this history daily as weapons against our stories being erased in the world or even worse, delivered to us offhandedly in the form of humor.
>
> As I interviewed relatives in both Ohio and Greenville, South Carolina, I began to piece together the story of my mother's life, my grandparents' lives, and the lives of cousins, aunts, and uncles. These stories, and the stories I had heard throughout my childhood, were told with the hope that I would carry on this family history and American history so that those coming after me could walk through the world as armed as I am.[5]

Clair Hughes has addressed the gleaning of sociological, cultural, and historical meaning from dress and appearance as represented in works of fiction. Hughes argues that "references to dress for both reader and writer contribute to the 'reality effect': they lend tangibility and visibility to character and context."[6] The role of descriptions of dress and appearance in creating visibility is particularly relevant to Woodson's work. In a *New York Times* opinion column, she articulated the intent of her work: to give young readers the opportunity to see themselves in the pages of her books. The inclusion of details regarding the dressing and appearance of hair effectively brings young readers directly into her experiences and helps them understand the historical roots of the black hair movement.

According to Howard's analysis, the core problem *brown girl dreaming* addresses is racism, but she also stresses the intentional projection of voice and visibility of African Americans living throughout Woodson's narrative as also central to the book's theme.[7] Joy Alexander, in exploring the emergence of verse novels in children's literature beginning in the late 1990s, argues that one of the core motivating features drawing authors to the genre is its ability to capture voice and provide an avenue for the expression of individual experiences and emotions. She also argues that the verse novel appeals to contemporary teens and preteens with its ties to simultaneous communication styles such as texting, as both offer writers and readers a first-person, telling it like it "really is" narrative with immediacy grounded in daily experiences.[8] Both Alexander and Howard stress the verse novel format's suitability to explore a core problem such as racism from a personal point of view as it is captured in *brown girl dreaming*. The semiotics of Black hair are interwoven throughout the book as a way to establish identity, community connectedness, and racial barriers and to change the world's social climate.

Woodson's verse novel is divided into five sections that capture her life from her birth in her father's home state of Ohio to her young years living with her mother's family in South Carolina, to her move to New York with her single mother, ending with the final two chapters capturing her beginnings as a young writer. A series of short poems titled "the listening verses" function throughout the book to slow down the narrative, allowing the reader to contemplate the meaning of each of the five sections. Howard stresses the role of these listening poems in encouraging reflection on the work's core themes of racism, achieving dreams, and the importance of family in so doing effectively functions as a "first step toward political advocacy" for the attentive reader.

PART 1: "I AM BORN"

The primary theme of race is introduced immediately in Jacqueline's birth narrative, along with information on the location where she came into the world. Each of the book's five sections is highly affected by its setting in the United States and its time period as the country is caught, as captured in this opening poem, "between Black and White":

I am born on a Tuesday at University Hospital
Columbus, Ohio,
USA—
A country caught
Between Black and White. (6)

The birth narrative of Jacqueline Woodson is continued and filled in by a poem titled "a girl named Jack," which introduces the family dynamics theme, both underscoring a strong tie to her father, her namesake, and also introducing the conflict between her parents that eventually leads to their separation and her move away from Ohio:

Good enough name for me, my father said
the day I was born.
Don't see why
she can't have it too.
But the women said no.
My mother first.
Then each aunt, pulling my pink blanket back
patting the crop of thick curls
tugging at my new toes
touching my cheek
We won't have a girl named Jack, my mother said. (6)

It is important to note that in this early and very central narrative, hair emerges as a key symbol of identity, with thick curls being a core signifier of the author's paternity.

PART 2: "THE STORIES OF SOUTH CAROLINA RUN LIKE RIVERS"

The book's second section focuses on Woodson's mother leaving her father in Ohio and moving the children to South Carolina to live with her parents. This return to the South is marked with a listening poem about racism as the children adjust to daily incidents of discrimination based on their racial identity:

How to listen # 2
In the stores downtown
We're always followed around
Just because we are brown. (82)

Dressing with care to combat racist responses from store clerks, bus drivers, schoolteachers, and other Southern Whites is a recurrent theme in this section. This narrative emerges most significantly for Jacqueline in the careful attention to dressing her and her siblings' hair by older family members. This theme of management of children's identity by older family members is first introduced in a poem capturing the act of her mother moving the family to the back of the bus as they entered the state of South Carolina in 1963:

greenville,
south carolina, 1963

On the bus, my mother moves with us to the back.
It is 1963
in South Carolina.
Too dangerous to sit closer to the front
and dare the driver
to make her move. Not with us. Not now.
Me in her arms all of three months old. My sister
and brother squeezed into the seat beside her. White
shirt, tie, and my brother's head shaved clean.
My sister's braids
white ribboned. (30)

Woodson captures the emphasis on managing children's hair within the Black community to ensure that they would be received and treated with respect both within the community and as they navigated through the surrounding dominant White cultural world. Erving Goffman's symbolic interaction program and review framework are helpful as a means of structuring the analysis, with female relatives managing the programs of Jacqueline Woodson and her siblings to best navigate their ways through White culture in South Carolina.[9]

The braiding and ribboning of Jacqueline and her older sister's hair by their grandmother is an act of both management of their identity for safety reasons and an act of love well recognized in the verse narrative in multiple poems in this section. In "the blanket," Woodson recalls the first time her mother left the children in South Carolina with her parents and went to New York City. Woodson remembers being surrounded by the warm weight of her grandparents' love during her mother's trip. Her grandfather, whom she refers to as Daddy Gunner, symbolically expresses his love by his weekly trip to the candy shop with his grandchildren; in contrast, their grandmother most often expresses her love by her attention to the girls' dress and appearance, particularly their hair:

It is Friday night and the weekend ahead
is already calling us
to the candy lady's house,
my hand in Daddy's
He doesn't know how to say no,
my grandmother's complains.
But neither does she,
dresses and socks and ribbons,
our hair pressed and curled.
She calls my sister and me her baby girls,

smiles proudly when the women say how pretty we are.
So the first time my mother goes to New York City
we don't know to be said, the weight
of our grandparents' love like a blanket
with us beneath it,
safe and warm. (78–79)

This section of the book devotes the most attention to the meaning of hair and hair management. One entire poem, "hair night," is dedicated to describing the Saturday night grooming ritual of hot hair combs, Dixie Peach hair grease, a horsehair brush, a parting stick, and a devoted, loving grandmother. During the slave era, enslaved peoples were not allowed to groom themselves daily.[10] They were given a short period for grooming during the week on Saturday night or early Sunday mornings to prepare to attend church later. This tradition of Saturday night hair preparation has been steadfast in the Black community.

Saturday night smells of biscuits and burning hair.
Supper done and my grandmother has transformed
the kitchen into a beauty shop. Laid across the table
is the hot comb, Dixie Peach hair grease,
horsehair brush, parting stick
and one girl at a time.
Jackie first my sister says,
our freshly washed hair damp
and spiraling over toweled shoulders
and pale cotton nightgowns. (83)

The semiotics of burning hair is directly related to the need for Blacks to assimilate to White beauty standards. Black women have been straightening their hair since slavery times. In the early days, they placed their heads on ironing boards while someone else passed a hot clothing iron over their hair; then, in the late 1900s, hot straightening combs became available to Black women thanks to entrepreneurs such as Annie Malone and Madame C. J. Walker.[11]

In "changes," while discussing the children's move to New York City with their mother, Woodson refers to her and her sister's hair rituals with their grandmother.

changes
Now the evenings are quiet with my mother gone
as though the night is listening

to the way we are counting the days. We know
even the feel of our grandmother's brush
being pulled through our hair
will fast become a memory. Those Saturday evenings
at her kitchen table, the smell
of Dixie Peach hair grease,
the sizzle of the straightening comb,
the hiss of the iron
against damp, newly washed ribbons, all of this
may happen again, but in another place. (108)

Woodson's memory of the signs her grandmother's love is linked to the hair ritual. Grooming her granddaughters' hair was one of the ways her she demonstrated her love. By this time in the book, the girls and their brother, Hope, had not been with their mother for several years. The thought of leaving the loving touch of her grandmother becomes too hard to bear.

It is also these ribbon memories that Jacqueline remembers rebelling against as she and her sister begin the path toward independent identity formation. These mixed emotions are captured in "ribbons," a poem late in this second section of the book:

ribbons
They are pale blue or pink or white.
They are neatly ironed each Saturday night.
Come Sunday morning, they are tied to the braids
hanging down past our ears.
We wear ribbons every day except Saturday
when we wash them by hand, Dell and I
side by side at the kitchen sink,
rubbing them with Ivory soap then rinsing them
beneath cool water.
Each of us
dreaming of the day our grandmother says
You're too old for ribbons.
But it feels like that day will never come.
When we hang them on the line to dry, we hope
they'll blow away in the night breeze
but they don't. Come morning, they're right
where we left them
gently moving in the cool air, eager to anchor us
to childhood. (121)

Ribbons are a sign of childhood, Jacqueline and Dell love the ritual of getting their hair washed, pressed, and braided, but in this stage of their lives (coming into adolescence and preadolescence), the girls are ready to leave the ribbons behind.

In part 2, "the stories of South Carolina run like rivers," readers are also introduced to beauty practices followed by Black women in the South. Jacqueline's mother moved among South Carolina, Ohio, and New York. As she transitioned between the North and the South, her hairstyles changed with her. During the 1960s, Black women in the South were "required" to straighten or press their hair. However, in the North, society was more liberal, and it was not uncommon for Black women to wear their hair in its natural state. At her mother's birthday party, held with her cousins to celebrate her return to South Carolina, the family is out doing the twist, and Woodson makes special note of her mother's new hairstyle:

I knew you weren't staying up North, the cousins say.
You belong here with us.
My mother throws her head back,
her newly pressed and curled hair gleaming
her smile the same one she had
before she left for Columbus.
She's MaryAnn Irby again. Georgiana and Gunner's
youngest daughter.
She's home. (34)

As background to this beauty practice of straightening Black textured hair, it is important to note that during the slave-era White masters had invented of "good" and "bad" Black hair as a way to cause an intraracial divide within the African slave community. The high status of Black slaves who more closely conformed to standards of White appearance, including being born with or able to display characteristics of "good hair," became deeply ingrained and normalized within the African Diaspora, as did the importance of conforming to "proper" female dress and appearance.[12] This fact was also stressed in Woodson's poems about women being trained to participate in the Civil Rights actions being orchestrated in the South.

Even my mother joins the fight.
When she thinks our grandmother
isn't watching she sneaks out
to meet the cousins downtown, but just as
she's stepping through the door,
her good dress and gloves on, my grandmother says,
Now don't go getting arrested. (73)

Just as Black children's hair was carefully coifed to help ensure they could safely navigate White dominant culture, young women working for Civil Rights were careful to model White standards in their dress and hairstyles for safety reasons. While this poem does not refer to Woodson's hair being straightened or pressed, it was likely pressed in keeping with unwritten beauty rules of the South.

PART 3: "FOLLOWED THE SKY'S MIRRORED CONSTELLATION TO FREEDOM"

The third section of the book tells the story of Jacqueline and her siblings moving to New York City to live with their mother. Not surprisingly, given the adjustment to leaving her grandparents and the South, this section delves into emotions related to loss. Her mother, busy with a new baby, struggles to keep up with her older children's the hair and dress needs after her sister's death. This poem captures how Jacqueline missed the rituals of Greenville, South Carolina, and her grandmother:

> This is what reminds of us Greenville,
> the Saturday-night pressing of satin ribbons
> Hope struggling with the knot in his tie,
> our hair oiled and pulled back into braids
> our mother's hands less sure
> than our grandmother's, the parts crooked, the braids
> coming undone. And now, Dell and I
> are left to iron our own dresses. (160)

Hairstyling is not just a ritual of grooming in the Black community; it symbolizes connection with others. In Africa, hairstyling has always been a sacred responsibility given only to family or close friends. In many tribes, the hair groomer assisted people with identifying their social status and rank. If one were a village chief, his hairstyle would be very different from the boy living in that same village.[13] Jacqueline uses memories of her maternal Aunt Kay braiding her hair to mourn the sudden loss of this aunt in an accident not long after their move to New York:

> Aunt Kay braiding my hair
> Aunt Kay running up the stairs to her own apartment
> And me running behind her.
> Aunt Kay laughing
> Aunt Kay hugging me.
> Then a fall.
> A crowd.

An ambulance.
My mother's tears.
A funeral.
And here, my Aunt Kay memories end. (150)

In many instances throughout the verse novel, hair is the trigger for a memory. In "our father, fading away," it also becomes a means of expressing the loss of memories of her father and her time in Ohio:

We forget the color of his skin—was it
Dark brown like mine or lighter like Dell's?
Did he have Hope and Dell's loose curls or my
Tighter, kinkier hair? (181)

The listening poem for this section hovers over and makes the reader consider one of the hardest losses captured in the book—the security and warmth of her grandparents' sanctuary of love in South Carolina. The children returned to South Carolina to live with their grandparents in the summer, but, due to Daddy Gunner's illness, their grandmother had to work full-time. As a result, Jacqueline and her siblings had to go to a daycare home, where they were bullied. Woodson captures the loss of the sanctuary of her grandmother's love and protection with a verse poem including the dramatic tearing away of her sister's newly ironed hair ribbons by other children at the daycare home:

My sister's tears are slow to come. But when they do,
it isn't sadness
It's something different that sends her swinging
her fists when
the others yank her braids until the satin,
newly ironed ribbons belong to them,
hidden away in the deep pockets of their dresses,
tucked into
their sagging stockings, buried inside their silver lunch pails.(194)

PART 4: "DEEP IN MY HEART, I DO BELIEVE"

The fourth section of the book, "deep in my heart, I do believe," charts the emergence of the Black Pride movement in American popular culture through the eyes of Jaqueline and her friends and family. The emergence of Black style linked to African roots during this period became political. It depicts the emergence of the Afro as both an aesthetic and political identity symbol in the Black community. Throughout the years the terminology used to refer to peoples of the African Diaspora in the United States transformed.

> The shift to calling oneself Black and being proud of it translated into a style that proudly hearkened back to Africa. More than skin color, the word became a political statement in terms of one's consciousness, color and culture. After generations of trying to neutralize distinctive African characteristics, people began to celebrate them. And just as hair had been central to the way Blacks of earlier years had sought to mainstream themselves, hair became a key determinant in visually declaring Black Pride.[14]

The Afro became a symbol of the fight for freedom; it was worn as a means of rebelling against mainstream ideologies about beauty. Not only political, the Afro was very trendy. Uncle Robert shows up on Jaqueline's doorstep with an Afro in a poem aptly titled "afros." Her mother also fashions her hair into an empowerment dome, much to the chagrin of her daughter, who wants to sport the style but is forbidden:

> Afros
> When Robert domes over with his hair blown out into
> an afro, I beg my mother
> for the same hairstyle.
> Everyone in the neighborhood
> Has one and all the black people on *Soul Train*. Even
> Michael Jackson and his brothers are all allowed to wear
> their hair this way.
> Even though she says no to me,
> my mom spends a lot of Saturday morning
> in her bedroom mirror,
> picking her own hair
> into a huge black and beautiful dome. (259)

Wearing an Afro in the late 1960s and 1970s was a sign of the revolution. It also permitted Whites to label Blacks as criminals or, worse, a member of the Black Panther Party.[15] Jacqueline's mother prohibited her children from wearing Afros out of protection rather than her being an unreasonable mother.

PART 5: "READY TO CHANGE THE WORLD"

The fifth section of the book poses Woodson as a young author on the cusp of making change and shows the reflection of that mindset in the world surrounding her. In "say it loud," Woodson captures the impact of the now more mature Black Pride movement with memories of the Black Panther organization as experienced within her family:

> My mother tells us the Black Panthers are doing
> all kinds of stuff
> to make the world a better place for Black children.
> In Oakland, they started a free breakfast program
> so that poor kids can have a meal
> before starting their school day. Pancakes,
> toast, eggs, fruit: we watch the kids eat happily,
> sing songs about how proud they are
> to be Black. We sing the song along with them
> stand on the bases of the lampposts and scream,
> *Say it loud: I'm Black and I'm proud until*
> my mother hollers from the window,
> *Get down before you break your neck.* (304)

In that same poem, Jaqueline talks about watching Angela Davis marching in California:

> Angela Davis smiles, gap-toothed and beautiful,
> raises her fist in the air
> says, *Power to the people, looks out from the television.* (305)

The impact of Angela Davis, and her signature Afro hairstyle, on Jacqueline and her friend Maria is dramatically marked by a "power to the people":

> On the TV screen a woman
> named Angela Davis is telling us
> there's a revolution going on and that it's time
> for Black people to defend themselves.
> So Maria and I walk through the streets,
> our fists raised in the air Angela Davis style.
> We read about her in the *Daily News*, run
> to the television each time she's interviewed.
> She is beautiful and powerful and has
> my same gap-toothed smile. We dream

of running away to California
to join the Black Panthers
the organization Angela is a part of.
She is not afraid, she says,
to die for what she believes in
but doesn't plan to die
without a fight. (302)

Even though Jaqueline's mother does not allow her to wear an Afro *or* listen to songs including the word *funk,* the author feels she is a part of the revolution, and she clearly states that her route into the action lies in writing the narrative:

When I hear the world word
revolution
I think of the carousel with
all those beautiful horses
going around as though they'll never stop and me
choosing the purple one each time, climbing up onto it
and reaching for the golden ring, as soft music plays.
The revolution is always going to be happening.

CONCLUSION

As we grapple with the dual challenges of updating children's literature and teaching history to children raised in the era of the immediate text message, the verse poem narrative prototype Woodson explores in *brown girl dreaming* offers a persuasive argument for both personal narrative and verse. Woodson's story situates contemporary discourse focused on Black hair within a relevant historical context for young and adult readers alike. Barbershops and beauty shops are community centers within African American neighborhoods in part linked to the history Woodson captures in this book. As we speak, ongoing discourse within African American families and communities continues to be focused on whether to embrace the natural hair movement or conform to patterns of hair straightening for work environments, with the pros and cons of both positions sometimes intensely debated. This novel in verse offers the young girl whose mother embraces the natural hair movement and whose auntie takes the same young girl to the beauty shop to have her hair straightened as a birthday gift a means of exploring her identity within an authentic historical context, helping her work her way to her expression of identity.

Woodson's work, with its poems focused on the effects of the surrounding dominant culture on a young African American girl, also provides reflective space for the same girl to make sense of contemporary controversies focused on African American hair. The recent banning of discrimination based on natural hairstyles in New York and California are news stories surrounding young Black children growing up in the United States.[16] During the same decade of this legislation, fashion runway shows featuring White models wearing locs have provoked often heated Twitter posts focused on the discrimination that Blacks often experience for wearing the same hairstyles.[17] In these same discussions, questions of cultural appropriation are raised with Black voices such as social activist bell hooks questioning the why behind appropriation, arguing that "within commodity culture, ethnicity becomes spice, seasoning that can liven up the dull dish that is mainstream white culture."[18] The final question focused on whether this runway performance showed respect for or colonized African American identity.[19] History and personal narrative are essential tools Woodson provides for young readers to make sense of these events and, on a deeper level, understand the significance of the news space these issues occupy in our cultural world.

Woodson's novel in verse, while important in the African American community, is also a meaningful work in helping those outside the community understand the deep and significant meaning of Black hair in the United States. The national controversy surrounding a White teacher's use of Carolivia Herron's children's book *Nappy Hair* in a third-grade classroom in Brooklyn in the 1990s underscored the importance of creating space for everyone to explore the history of Black hairstyles in the United States to effectively educate children across racial lines to support each other and understand the world they are living in.[20] In response to the controversy, Herron, the African American writer of *Nappy Hair* defended her book by stating that she intended to reclaim and celebrate the historically derogatory word *nappy* to celebrate Black natural hair. Despite her statement, Black parents of children in the Brooklyn classroom remained offended by the book and its illustrations. Ultimately, the White teacher was moved to a different school district. Black hair's history is so complex and painful that even when a White person tries to advocate for Blacks, it can be interpreted as mockery and, thus, be taken the wrong way

The emergence of hair as a central theme in this book of memories points to the importance of paying close attention to Black hair as a symbol and instrument of change as we move toward justice in the United States. While rooted in the past, its meaning continually evolves and moves us into future identities and new worldviews.

NOTES

1. Jacqueline Woodson, *brown girl dreaming* (New York: Nancy Paulsen Books, 2014). Further citations of this work are given in the text.
2. Isabel Wilkerson, *The Warmth of Other Suns: The Epic Story of America's Great Migration* (New York: Vintage, 2010).
3. Krystal Howard, "Collage, Confessional, and Crisis in Jacqueline Woodson's *brown girl dreaming*," *Children's Literature Association Quarterly* 42, no. 3 (2017): 326–44.
4. Jacqueline Woodson, "The Pain of the Watermelon Joke," *New York Times*, Nov. 28, 2014.
5. Woodson, "The Pain of the Watermelon Joke."
6. Clair Hughes, *Dressed in Fiction* (New York: Berg, 2005), 2.
7. Howard, "Collage, Confessional, and Crisis."
8. Joy Alexander, "The Verse-Novel: A New Genre," *Children's Literature in Education* 36, no. 3 (2005): 269–83.
9. Erving Goffman, *The Presentation of Self in Everyday Life* (New York: Overlook, 1959).
10. Shane White and Graham White, "Slave Hair and African American Culture in the Eighteenth and Nineteenth Centuries," *Journal of Southern History* 61, no. 1 (1995): 45–76.
11. Willie L. Morrow, *400 Years without a Comb: The Untold Story*, 3rd ed. (San Diego: California Curl, a Division of Morrow's Unlimited, 1990).
12. Ayana D. Byrd and Lori L. Tharps, *Hair Story: Untangling the Roots of Black Hair in America*, 2nd. ed. (New York: St. Martin's, 2014); Tameka N. Ellington, "Social Networking Sites: A Support System for African American Women Wearing Natural Hair," *International Journal of Fashion Design, Technology, and Education* 8, no. 1 (2015): 21–29; Eletra S. Gilchrist and Courtney Thompson, "African-American Women's Perceptions of Constitutive Meanings of Good Hair Articulated in Black Hair Magazine Advertisements," *Journalism and Mass Communications* 2, no. 1 (2012): 279–93.
13. Byrd and Tharps, *Hair Story*, 4.
14. Byrd and Tharps, *Hair Story*.
15. Byrd and Tharps, *Hair Story*.
16. Stacey Stowe, "New York City to Ban Discrimination Based on Hair," *New York Times*, Feb. 18, 2019; Liam Stack, "California Is First State to Ban Discrimination Based on Natural Hair," *New York Times*, June 28, 2019.
17. Valeriya Safronova, "Marc Jacobs's Use of Faux Locs on Models Draws Social Media Ire," *New York Times*, Sept. 16, 2016.
18. bell hooks, "Eating the Other: Desire and Resistance," in *Black Looks: Race and Representation* (Boston: South End Press, 1992), 21–39.
19. Alexander Fury, "Marc Jacobs and the Appropriateness of Appropriation," *New York Times*, Sept. 19, 2016.
20. Lynette Holloway, "Crew Defends Teacher in Book Dispute," *New York Times*, Dec. 15, 1998; Ingrid Banks, *Hair Matters: Beauty, Power, and Black Women's Consciousness* (New York: New York Univ. Press, 2000).

PART 2

Critical Race Theory and a Sociocognitive Approach to Perceptions of Black Hair

CHAPTER 3

"Don't Need a Trip to the Beauty Shop"

DEPICTIONS OF AFRO-TEXTURED HAIR IN CHILDREN'S MEDIA

Tameka N. Ellington and Annette Lynch

Children are taught from an early age whether they have "good" hair or "bad" hair. When African American babies are born, their parents inspect them to make sure they have all their fingers and toes, like parents of any race. Then they look at their newborn babies' potential skin color, which can be estimated based on the color of the baby's ears. And as Ayana Byrd and Lori Tharps report, "relatives speculate over the texture of hair that will cover the baby's head, and the loaded objectives 'good' and 'bad' are already in the air."[1] The quality of hair texture is harder to predict because hair texture is determined by genetics; however, genes do not always give accurate predictions. There is always hope, and some might say, "I hope my baby keeps her 'good' hair. It lays down so nice and is so slick and soft!" As the baby ages, her true hair texture begins to appear, and this leaves some parents disappointed.

At a young age, girls begin drawing conclusions about the value of their hair; children as early as five years old are becoming aware of culturally ideal beauty and body standards.[2] Parents unconsciously inflict damage on their children's self-esteem when they classify them as having "good" or "bad" hair. The children with "good" hair are praised and will often "continue to engage in the oppressive distinction that leads to the perpetuation of those beliefs."[3] What role does the media targeted at African American children play in upholding the ideology of "good" and "bad" hair?

Colorism, discussed in depth in chapter 1, is closely connected to *texturism,* coined by Tameka Ellington. Both are rooted in slavery and discrimination. Light-skinned African Americans were the offspring of White masters or their sons, who had forced copulation with their female slaves. These children grew up with access to better clothing, food, and living conditions than their darker-skinned kin. Sometimes, the master's offspring lived in the "big house" with them—hence, the term *house negro.* Along with the children's light skin, their hair texture was much straighter and closer to that of White people's hair; thus, it was perceived as "better." Meanwhile, the slaves with dark skin and kinky hair remained in the field and rarely had access to the privileges of their lighter counterparts.[4]

Prejudices based on skin color and hair texture run blood deep and are still very prevalent, because they have a basis in some truth. Understandably, the master's children, whether White or biracial, had educational opportunities, something field slaves were forbidden. Some Black people even tried to "pass" for White so that they could escape and have better lives. "Straight hair translated to economic opportunity and social advantage." Hair texture was always the true test, because some light-skinned slaves had kinkier hair. The straighter the hair, the closer to White that person was.[5] The "good" versus "bad" hair concept caused lasting intracultural tension and disdain among African Americans.

Wanda Brooks and Jonda McNair have employed content analysis to evaluate six picture books written by African American authors and found that three themes surrounding hair emerged: "(1) the perspective that all hair is good, (2) the connection between Black hair and African American history, and (3) the bonding of females while hair is being combed and/or styled."[6] These themes represent authors whose goal is to enhance cultural understanding and acceptance among their audience. Enforcing and/or reinforcing the belief that *all* hair is good is a shared responsibility that many African American authors who discuss Black culture accept. Their books and articles serve as a platform for countering the notion that Afro-textured or Black hair is less attractive than straight hair.

The concept of Black hair cannot be discussed without mentioning its history, because the great disdain that African Americans and other Blacks of the diaspora have regarding their hair is a direct result of slavery and colonization. bell hooks said it best: "Real good hair is straight hair, hair like white folks' hair. Yet, no one says so. No one says your hair is so nice, so beautiful because it is like white folks' hair. We pretend that the standards we measure our beauty by are our own invention."[7] Because such negativity surrounds the topic of Black hair, hair salons or areas near the kitchen sink or stove create a space where African American women and girls can come together and express their spiritual and mental hurts regarding their self-identities. The comradery that occurs while women are getting their hair done has historical roots in early West African societies, in which hairstyles symbolized status regarding wealth, marital state, ethnic group, and social rank. Hair grooming was (and still is) a sacred and intimate affair. In the early years, the hairdresser was valued as a master of their art and was only allowed to do the hair of someone of the same sex.[8] The cultural glory that was Black hair came to a screeching halt when Africans were forced to assimilate White beauty standards.

THE PERPETUAL WHITE STANDARD OF BEAUTY IN CHILDREN'S MEDIA

Nancy Wang Yuen's 2016 research suggests that prolonged television exposure causes a decrease in self-esteem for all girls and Black boys. However, she found that prolonged television exposure has an inverse effect on White boys, increasing their self-esteem. "These differences correlate with the racial and gender practices in Hollywood, which predominantly casts White men as heroes while erasing or subordinating other groups as villains, sidekicks, and sexual objects."[9] As is other media, children's media is controlled by White men, who mostly feature White ways of life, void of diversity and inclusion.[10] White media pushes and enforces White standards of beauty; African American children often do not see themselves in the media they are consuming. *Symbolic annihilation,* a term George Gerbner and Larry Gross coined in 1976, provides a research framework focusing on the absence of underrepresented peoples in the media.[11]

In 1978, Gaye Tuchman divided symbolic annihilation into three parts: omission, trivialization, and condemnation. These aspects not only vilify communities of identity but make members invisible through the explicit lack of representation in all forms of media, including film, song, books, news media, and visual art.[12]

In American society, the physical appearances of African Americans are perceived as inferior or less than those of White Americans. Therefore, it is normal and necessary for creators of African American children's literature and other media to emphasize that Black is indeed beautiful, particularly regarding hair.[13] Media targeted toward children does not escape the grips of politics in our country. Similar to adult media, children's media often represents more significant societal issues—such as racism.

Disney, one of the largest producers of cartons and films targeted to preschool and primary school–aged girls, has been criticized for the lack of diversity in its productions.[14] The 2013 phenomenon *Frozen* has been called out for Whitewashing the characters inspired by the Sámi indigenous people of Scandinavia (who were of Asian descent).[15] An artist using the Tumblr handle Juliajm15 took matters into her own hands and drew the characters Elsa and Anna as Black women. Many of Juliajm15's fans praised the work. "I just wanted to say that I'm black, and I showed my baby cousin the Elsa that you posted, and she has been obsessed with black Elsa ever since and prefers her to the original because 'she's just like me.' Thank you for standing up for minorities."[16]

Disney continues attempting to make amends for its traditionally racially-insensitive products and media. Journalist Alice Jones writes, "It took [them] 70 years and 49 films before girls of colour finally got a princess who looked like them in 2009s 'The Princess and the Frog.'"[17] However, critics would not allow Disney to come off unscathed just because it finally had a Black princess. Critics of *The Princess and the Frog* have pointed to Tiana's love interest, Prince Naveen, as the movie's biggest problem: he is ethnically ambiguous. Naveen's home country, Maldonia, is left unexplained, and his accent is confusing and difficult to place. "It's been suggested that these are all devices used by Disney so that they didn't have to have an identifiably black male playing a king i.e., in a position of power."[18]

Again, in an attempt to right its wrongs, Disney announced it was remaking *The Little Mermaid* as a live-action movie. In the new version, Ariel, the little mermaid, is not a red-haired White character; rather, singer and actress Halle Bailey—an African American wearing locs—is the new Ariel. This is significant for several reasons: First, Bailey is African American. Second, the movie will be live-action, so children can really see themselves in this character. And third, Bailey's hair is not long and chemically straightened (the mainstream preference); her hair is in its natural state. Many non–African American Disney fans have been in an uproar about this and voiced their contempt by starting the #NotMyAriel movement. "The reaction to Bailey's casting only underlines its importance."[19]

SESAME STREET: THE PROGRESSIVE EXAMPLE FOR CHILDREN'S MEDIA

In contrast to Disney, The Children's Television Workshop (renamed Sesame Workshop in 2000) was deliberate in representing diversity from the start of *Sesame Street* in 1969. Activist and founding president of the Black Psychiatrists of America Chester Pierce, noticed that in the wake of the death of Dr. Martin Luther King Jr., 95 percent of families in America had television sets at home. Pierce was extremely concerned with television's influence on children's minds, because television shows had previously been devoid of people of color. Television had been used as a means of solidifying the United States' racist milieu. In his research, Pierce discovered that even after the Civil Rights Law was passed, African Americans faced racism; however, this was more subtle and indirect than typical in-your-face racism. Pierce coined the term *microaggressions* to describe the marginalization African Americans felt, and still feel today. Television producers who planned to rectify the inherent racism asked Pierce to serve as senior advisor for their new show, *Sesame Street*.[20]

In 2017, *HuffPost* published an article praising *Sesame Street* for eleven key moments when it "championed diversity and inclusion." Those instances highlight the program's racially and ethnically diverse cast, its characters' differing abilities, children coping with having an incarcerated parent, characters dealing with death, and characters expressing love for their curly, Afro-textured hair.[21] Critics were concerned about *Sesame Street*'s diversity mission and the racial nature of its "hidden curriculum" from the very beginning. In May 1970, a statewide commission in Mississippi secretly voted to have the show taken off the air. It claimed that some legislators were not "ready" to see that much diversity in a cast. However, the state reversed the decision after the "secret" vote made national news. *Sesame Street* was, and in many ways remains, the most progressive children's show. Journalist Anne Harrington wrote, "What mattered most about Sesame Street was not the alphabet songs, the counting games, or the funny puppets. What mattered most was its vision of an integrated society where everyone was a friend and treated with respect."[22] Based on the articles just discussed, the following question guided the current research study: "What types of media messages are preschool and primary-age African American girls exposed to regarding their hair? To what degree are these messages promoting a positive or negative self-image for African American girls regarding their hair?"

THEORETICAL FRAMEWORK

In 2018, the number of African American women wearing their natural hair texture was 40 percent, with the remaining 60 percent wearing straightened hairstyles.[23] The fact that most African American women believe straightened hair is more beautiful may result from African *psychological misorientation,* the condition that occurs whenever African-centered consciousness is depleted due to stereotypical and/or negative images in mass media.[24] The brainwashing effects of slavery and colonization are still evident in the beauty industry; therefore, the authors have employed a critical race theory (CRT) framework to provide a better understanding of media messages' influence on African American women and girls. The CRT model focuses on a commitment to social justice and addresses the centrality of race, racism, and their intersectionality. It emphasizes the importance of examining and attempting to understand the sociocultural forces that shape how we and others perceive, experience, and respond to racism. A CRT lens combats the idea that racism is normal and helps to deconstruct societal microaggressive racism, which is more difficult to detect.[25] A CRT lens will make plain discriminatory or oppressive content in the media and help tell the story of possible resulting African psychological misorientation the girls may be suffering regarding their Afro-textured hair. From a CRT perspective, the media (and the White men who run it) has the power to assist in changing society's negative view of Afro-textured hair and fostering cultural validation in African American girls.

Methods

For the current study, a qualitative inductive methodology was employed, allowing for content analysis to be conducted with open-coded data. The aim was to develop categories and abstractions with the end result of defining themes in the research.[26] Inductive content analysis allows researchers to identify patterns of meaning as a representation of the data. Also, this form of data analysis will enable researchers to evaluate documents and media in areas with limited or new knowledge.[27]

Sample

The sample consisted of five television shows, one online game, one feature-length film, one short film, six books, and one music video (see Table 1). Search terms used to find the sample included cartoons about Black girls' hair, books on Black hair, positive children's media about hair, negative children's media about hair, and African American girls in cartoons. The criteria for the media selected for this study required that each was marketed toward African American preschool and primary–school aged girls, referred to hair, featured at least one African American girl, and was produced after the natural hair movement began in the early 2000s.

The global phenomenon that is the natural hair movement took shape as a result of social media, products, and many books that were created due to the lack of support and knowledge African American women had regarding their Afro-textured hair. Most of these African American women had not seen their natural hair texture since they were young, typically between six and twelve years of age, when most had similar rites of passage: they had their hair chemically straightened, and it has been straight ever since.

Table 1. Description of Sample

Study Sample of Media Targeted Toward Preschool and Primary-Aged Children

No.	Media Genre	Year	Author/Producer	Title
1	TV Show	2010	Sesame Street	I Love My Hair
2	TV Show	2018	Sesame Street	Hair Training
3	TV Show	2009	Sesame Street	Whoopi's Skin Elmo's Fur
4	TV Show	2014	Disney's Doc McStuffins	Take Your Doc to Work Day
5	TV Show	2004	Nickelodeon's Winx Club	Miss Magix
6	Online game	2014	Nick Jr.'s Bubble Guppies	Good Hair Day
7	Movie	2014	Sony Pictures	Annie
8	Short film	2019	Sony Pictures by Matthew A. Cherry	Hair Love
9	Book	2015	Natalie McGriff and Angie Nixon	The Adventures of Moxie Girl
10	Book	2014	Tina Olajide and Courtney Bernard	Emi's Curly, Coily, Cotton Candy Hair
11	Book	1999	bell hooks and Chris Raschka	Happy to be Nappy
12	Book	2013	Alonda Williams and Tyrus Goshay	Penny and the Magic Puffballs
13	Book		Ladosha Wright and Larry Tinsley	Curly Hair Adventures
14	Book	2013	Aya de León	Puffy People Whose Hair Defies Gravity
15	Book	2013	Crystal Swain-Bates	Big Hair Don't Care
16	Music video	2010	Roc Nation by Willow Smith	Whip My hair

So from their childhoods until they went natural, most African American women know only that chemically straightened version of their hair. They had no sense of how their true hair texture feels or looks.

As a result of the natural hair movement, Afro-textured hair has become mainstream, no longer associated only with Black radicals and Rastafarians. Fifteen to twenty years into the natural hair movement, women with their natural hair texture are featured in television ads, leading television networks, and big films, whereas early, the media favored only African Americans with features that fit within the White standard of beauty. The natural hair movement set the precedent for the community engagement, support, education, and economic growth of African American women wearing their hair naturally.[28]

Data Analysis

The first phase of the analysis was the content-coding scheme development, and the second was the creation of content classifications for pattern analysis and frequencies. Codes were based on themes that emerged from the data. A matrix was developed to record the purpose of the media message, the number of African American girls featured, the hair texture each girl had, the type of hairstyle each girl wore, and the tone of the message.

André Walker, a hair stylist to Oprah Winfrey, devised a numbering system to help women define their hair texture and promote better hair care practices. Type 1a is the straightest hair, and type 4b is the kinkiest hair texture. Detailing the hair texture and styling is important to note because African American girls have always been taught that they must "tame" Afro-textured hair—usually classified as type 4.

Results: Types of Messages

The research questions guiding the study asked, "What types of media messages are preschool and primary age African American girls exposed to regarding their hair? To what degree are media messages promoting a positive self-image for African American girls regarding their hair?" The data revealed five main themes across all genres: first, happily celebrating Afro-textured hair; second, encouraging self-love and self-acceptance; third, educating girls about their hair; fourth, showing styling options; fifth, discussing the various types of Afro-textured hair, and sixth, examining negative media messages.

Celebrating Afro-Textured Hair

The media shows happy characters dancing around, laughing, and/or singing. The mood is upbeat, and the settings bright and colorful. Children's media usually carries a happy or celebratory tone, and the sample in the current study was no exception. In the sample, 87 percent feature a happy or celebratory tone regarding the girls' hair. Just as in the research conducted by Brooks and McNair, the current study includes a blanket message that all hair is "good" hair.[29] "Good" is addressed and discussed as healthy and versatile instead of straight and long, simulating dominant beauty ideals.

> Hair to take the gloom away.
> These short tight naps or plaited strands
> All let girls go running free.

This short stanza from author bell hooks's children's book *Happy to Be Nappy* describes what good hair really is—freedom. The *Sesame Street* "I Love My

Hair" episode and the music video for Willow Smith's song "Whip My Hair" are great examples of jubilant messages about Black hair.

Encouraging Self-Acceptance and Self-Love

Media classified as encouraging self-love/acceptance had descriptive terminology to describe hair as "beautiful" (Tina Olajide's *Emi's Curly, Coily, Cotton Candy Hair*) or "magic" (Natalie McGriff, *The Adventures of Moxie Girl*, and Alonda Williams, *Penny and the Magic Puffballs*). The message of self-love runs through 81 percent of the media. The main purpose of much of the media is to promote self-love and cultural awareness. African Americans and other Blacks of the diaspora have faced more cultural hate (psychological misorientation) than other cultures, due to the institutionalized racism that spans the globe. Willow Smith's celebratory "Whip My Hair" promotes self-love.

> Don't let haters keep me off my grind
> With my head up, I know I'll be fine
> Keep fighting until I get there
> When I'm down and I feel like giving up
> I think again
> I whip my hair back and forth

"Whip My Hair" is a metaphor for activating a young girl's spunky nature, self-confidence, determination, and resilience. Natalie McGriff, seven-year-old author of *The Adventures of Moxie Girl*, was not always proud of her Afro-textured hair, so her mother encouraged her to write about it. McGriff submitted her comic book concept at the One Spark entrepreneurial festival in 2015 and won $16,000, with the promise to encourage other girls to love their hair. The "I Love My Hair" segment on *Sesame Street* features an African American Muppet with Afro-textured hair who sang, "Don't need a trip to the beauty shop, cuz I like what I got on top!" This statement refers to the rites of passage for African American girls having their Afro-textured hair chemically straightened at the hair salon for the first time. Being a business entity also, *Sesame Street* saw "I Love My Hair" as a money-making opportunity and another avenue to promote self-love, with t-shirts featuring Shirley, the "I Love My Hair" Muppet. At the end of her book *Curly Hair Adventures*, author Ladosha Wright leaves room for each of her young readers to draw a self-portrait inside of a beautiful frame, and next to their portraits is the following poem, which Wright encourages readers to recite:

> I am special.
> I am smart.
> I can be anything I want to be.

I love myself. I love my hair.
It is a unique part of me.

Educating Girls about Their Hair

Only 25 percent of the media focused on educating African American girls about their hair. This finding is surprising, because education is the first step to acceptance. The more you know about your hair, the deeper you can love it and accept it exactly as it is.

Emi's Curly, Coily, Cotton Candy Hair by Tina Olajide takes the reader on a step-by-step hair washing routine, from shampooing, conditioning, and detangling, to, finally, twisting. Matthew A. Cherry's movie short *Hair Love* is a silent film of a father learning to care for his daughter's hair through adorably funny trial and error. *Sesame Street* had an educational focus for two of its three segments on hair: "Whoopi's Skin and Elmo's Fur" and "Hair Training," where an African American Muppet, Gabrielle, plays with her White Muppet friend, Prairie Dawn. As they play and dance, they realize that their hair does not move the same way. Gabrielle wears Afro puffs and Prairie Dawn wears hers long and straight. Disappointed, the girls go to Gina, an adult on the show, and Prairie Dawn asks Gina if she could style her hair in Afro puffs like Gabrielle's. The *Sesame Street* writers are so clever that they often write messages within their messages. It is important to note that Prairie Dawn wants her hair like Gabrielle's, not the other way around, as African Americans are typically forced to fit within the White standard of beauty.

Styling Options for Afro-Textured Hair

The researchers evaluated the hairstyles worn by the characters featured in the media. The three most popular styles for African American girls were the Afro, Afro puffs, and braids. Fifty percent of the sample focused on displaying various styling options for girls' hair. In the children's television program *Doc McStuffins*, the main character, Dottie McStuffins, pretends to be the doctor of her stuffed animals and dolls. In the episode included in the study, one of Doc's dolls does not like her super "Curly-Q" hair texture. Through song and dance, Doc and her stuffed animal friends show the doll how versatile and great her hair really is.

Nickelodeon's Good Hair Day game, featuring *Bubble Guppies* characters, provides a fun way for children to explore styling options for all hair textures, including a cornrow hairstyle. Cornrows, which originated in African cultures, have a long history.[30] bell hooks's book *Happy to Be Nappy* depicts a beautifully painted range of hair shapes and styles. The "I Love My Hair" episode of *Sesame Street* shows a Muppet character wearing an Afro, cornrows, box or plait braids, locs, puffballs, and a large bow. In the music video for "Whip My Hair," Willow Smith wears box braids, an Afro-puff mohawk, and Bantu knots—all styles rooted in West African tradition. Featuring these styling options is significant because it allows African American girls to see that their hair is versatile and special, not at all the burden it is portrayed as in much of popular media.

Celebrating Various Textures of Hair

Until the 1960s when they started producing their own media, African Americans were not shown on television or in other forms of media, unless they held subordinate positions. Once African Americans began appearing more regularly in mainstream media, those people who aligned closer to the White standard of beauty were the only African Americans being featured unless, again, there was a subordinate role to be filled. Therefore, it was important that the present study evaluate the hair texture (with grades of curl and texture) and style of the African American girls shown in the sample. Seventy-five percent of the media featured girls with 4a or 4b textured hair. This is significant, but it may also be due to the fact that most preschool and primary-aged girls do not wear perms or straighteners, weaves, wigs, or other African American women's hairstyles frequently shown in the media.

Of the media discussed, 37 percent discussed hair-texture differences. Aya de Léon's book *Puffy: People Whose Hair Defies Gravity* features photography with people who have various textures of "puffy" hair. The photos give accurate examples of what hair texture looks like, from 3a to 4b hair. Wright's *Curly Hair Adventures* takes the reader on a fantasy trip around the world, where the main character, Rose, meets people of various nationalities who have diverse types of hair textures. *Sesame Street*'s episode featuring Whoopi Goldberg with the Muppet Elmo helps children understand that there are differences in skin color and hair (or fur) texture. The segment ends with Elmo asking Whoopi if he can trade hair with her because he likes her hair so much. Whoopi replies, "You can't trade things like hair. . . . And even if we could trade, I wouldn't want to. I like my skin and I like my hair, and I'd like to keep them both."

Examining Negative Media Messages

Eighteen percent of the media had negative messages associated with Afro-textured hair. Two negative comments were stated in the form of a joke and microaggressive dialogue. A CRT lens helps in recognizing the subtle nature in these harmful comments. The book *Big Hair Don't Care*, by Crystal Swain-Bates, straddles positive and negative media messages. The main character's hair (worn in an Afro) is referred to as a cotton ball, a hat, and a wall blocking the view for others.

I've got big hair, my friend does too
And at the movies and the zoo
It often blocks out all the view
So never sit behind us two.

This stanza is problematic because it stigmatizes Afro-textured hair as a societal burden.

The movie *Annie* was remade in 2014 with an African American girl, Quvenzhané Wallis, cast as the lead. The African American community was thrilled because this classic movie would cross social boundaries. Unfortunately, it includes negative references to Annie's hair, calling it big and wild. In this instance, Annie is watching a herself on the news being rescued by the lead male character, Will Stacks, played by Jamie Foxx. While watching the news footage, Annie exclaims in disbelief, "Whoa, my hair is gigantic." In another scene in the movie, Miss Hannigan, who runs the orphanage, mocks Annie by impersonating her voice and moving her hands in and out in reference to Annie's hair size. Again, this message perpetuates the ideology that Afro-textured hair is a nuisance. As mentioned earlier, African American women are often told to tame their wild, unprofessional hair.[31]

Winx Club, a Nickelodeon television show, provides the study's second example of a negative media message about Afro-textured hair. Episode 12 of the first season, broadcast in 2012, features a scene where the characters are getting dressed for a big event. Two girls, assisting the White blonde lead character with her hair, commented that it is like "gold silk." In another room, the Black character is in tears because her straightened hair has curled back into its natural Afro state. She continues to cry as the other girls look on, one calling her hair a "catastrophe," while another girl touches her hair, causing it to bounce back like a spring. The blond character looks around the corner to see what the fuss is about, and when she sees the Black girl's Afro hair, she panics: "What is that?" This comment sends the Black girl running down the hall and crying in despair. When critics learned about this clip of *Winx Club*, it went viral and was posted on several social media sites, including Black Entertainment Television's website (BET.com). Critics commented about the racist nature of the show and how it should be taken off the air.[32]

CONCLUSION

In the present study, 87 percent of the media sample targeted at African American preschool and primary-age girls was positive and focused on celebrating Afro-textured hair, building self-acceptance, educating the girls, showing various styling options, and discussing the various types of Afro-textured hair. Of the entire sample, *Sesame Street* has the most progressive messages. It depicts Muppets as African American girls taking pride in their hair and showing the versatility of hair as a medium of expression. The show also takes advantage of celebrity recognition to confer the message that all hair (and fur, for that matter!) is beautiful. These messages are very powerful, because media still tells girls their hair is unmanageable, unattractive, and "bad."

Books and other media are essential to the development of children's literacy and self-esteem—specifically self-esteem regarding their hair texture. African American authors, filmmakers, and artists are working to boost cultural pride and awareness in children with their self-affirming media. Researchers Wanda Brooks and Jonda McNair wrote, "Children's books [and other media] should serve as mirrors and windows, therefore allowing children to see images of themselves and others in the books they read [and media they consume]."[33]

Collecting data for this study involved a laborious process to find media discussing African American hair. The researchers were hoping to locate commercials featuring toys or other products that mentioned Afro-textured hair and fit the other study criteria, but there were none. Future research may delve deeper in the data of media influences via interviews or focus groups with girls regarding perceptions of their hair. Another avenue would include combing the *Sesame Street* archives more carefully in an ethnographic case study to evaluate the show's other sociocultural messages. Further content analysis research regarding the messages Black girls get in school spaces regarding their hair will give a well-rounded look at girls' day-to-day experiences. Black girls still often face discrimination in school. In 2021, Jimmy Hoffmeyer, a Michigan parent of a Black girl, filed a lawsuit against his daughter's teacher for cutting her hair without permission.[34] The current study contributes to the further understanding of African American culture, particularly racial body image disparities related to hair.

NOTES

1. Ayana D. Byrd and Lori L. Tharps, *Hair Story: Untangling the Roots of Black Hair in America*, 2nd ed. (New York: St. Martin's, 2014), 134.
2. Linda Smolak, "Body Image in Children and Adolescents: Where Do We Go from Here?," *Body Image* 1 (Jan. 2004): 15–28.
3. Ingrid Banks, *Hair Matters: Beauty, Power, and Black Women's Consciousness* (New York: New York Univ. Press, 2000).
4. Byrd and Tharps, *Hair Story.*
5. Byrd and Tharps, *Hair Story*, 17.
6. Wanda Brooks and Jonda McNair, "'Combing' Through Representations of Black Girls' Hair in African American Children's Literature," *Children's Literature in Education* 46, no. 3 (2015): 302.

7. bell hooks, "From Black Is a Woman's Color," *Callaloo* 39 (Spring 1989): 382–88.
8. Tameka N. Ellington, "Natural Hair," in *Berg Encyclopedia of World Dress and Fashion,* ed. Joanne B. Eicher and Doran H. Ross (New York: Oxford Univ. Press, 2015).
9. Nancy Wang Yuen, *Reel Inequality: Hollywood Actors and Racism* (New Brunswick, NJ: Rutgers Univ. Press, 2016).
10. Christy LaPierre, "Mass Media in the White Man's World," *Edge—Ethics of Development in a Global Environment,* Stanford Univ., June 4, 1999, https://web.stanford.edu/class/e297c/poverty_prejudice/mediarace/mass.htm.
11. George Gerbner and Larry Gross. "Living with Television: The Violence Profile," *Journal of Communication* 26, no. 2 (1976): 172–99.
12. Gaye Tuchman, "Making News: A Study in the Construction of Reality," *Social Forces* 59 (1978): 1341–42.
13. Brooks and McNair, "'Combing' Through Representations of Black Girls' Hair," 300.
14. Kat George, "The Disney Movies You Grew Up with Are Incredibly Racist," *VH1 News,* Jan. 9, 2015, http://www.vh1.com/news/310/racist-disney-movies/.
15. Embi Ussir, "Disney's *Frozen* Whitewashing Controversy," *Know Your Meme,* 2014, https://knowyourmeme.com/memes/events/disneys-frozen-whitewashing-controversy.
16. Jessica Arnold, "What *Frozen*'s Anna and Elsa Would Look Like if They Were Black," *Sheknows.com,* Feb. 6, 2015, https://www.sheknows.com/entertainment/articles/1072729/what-frozens-anna-and-elsa-would-look-like-if-they-were-black-photos/.
17. Alice Jones, "A Black Little Mermaid Played by Halle Bailey Is a Cause for Celebration, not Complaining," *iNews,* July 4, 2019, https://inews.co.uk/culture/little-mermaid-halle-bailey-ariel-remake-controversy-499213.
18. George, "Disney Movies You Grew Up with Are Incredibly Racist."
19. Jones, "Black Little Mermaid Played by Halle Bailey."
20. Anne Harrington, "'Sesame Street' Was a Radical Experiment in Challenging Institutional Racism," *Quartz,* May 25, 2019, https://qz.com/1626488/sesame-street-began-as-an-experiment-in-challenging-racism/.
21. Taylor Pittman, "11 Moments On 'Sesame Street' That Championed Diversity and Inclusion," *Huffpost.com,* updated Feb. 7, 2018, https://www.huffpost.com/entry/moments-on-sesame-street-that-championed-diversity-and-inclusion_n_58d5257ae4b03787d3576ba9.
22. Harrington, "'Sesame Street' Was a Radical Experiment."
23. "Naturally Confident: More Than Half of Black Women Say Their Hair Makes Them Feel Beautiful," Mintel Press Office website, Oct. 9, 2018, https://www.mintel.com/press-centre/beauty-and-personal-care/naturally-confident-more-than-half-of-black-women-say-their-hair-makes-them-feel-beautiful.
24. Daudi Ajani ya Azibo, "Criteria That Indicates When African Centered Consciousness Is Endangered or Depleted by the Mass Media," *Journal of Pan-African Studies* 3, no. 8 (2010): 135–50.
25. Daniel Solórzano, Miguel Ceja, and Tara Yosso, "Critical Race Theory, Racial Microaggressions, and Campus Racial Climate: The Experiences of African American College Students," *Journal of Negro Education* 69, nos. 1–2 (2000): 60–73.
26. Satu Elo and Helvi Kyngäs, "The Qualitative Content Analysis Process," *Journal of Advanced Nursing* 62, no. 1 (2008): 107–15.

27. Brooks and McNair, "'Combing' Through Representations of Black Girls' Hair."

28. Tameka N. Ellington, "Social Networking Sites: A Support System for African American Women Wearing Natural Hair," *Journalism and Mass Communication* 4, no. 9 (2014): 21–29.

29. Brooks and McNair, "'Combing' Through Representations of Black Girls' Hair."

30. Tameka Ellington, "Corn Rows," in Eicher and Ross, *Berg Encyclopedia of World Dress and Fashion*, 1–5.

31. Banks, *Hair Matters*.

32. Veronica Wells, "'Winx Club' and When Cartoons Teach Our Children to Hate Their Hair," *MadameNoire*, June 2, 2016, https://madamenoire.com/700103/winx-club-and-when-cartoons-teach-our-children-to-hate-their-hair/.

33. Brooks and McNair, "'Combing' Through Representations of Black Girls' Hair."

34. "Michigan Father Files $1M Suit after Teacher Cuts His Biracial Daughter's Hair," *Associated Press*, Sept. 17, 2021, https://www.nbcnews.com/news/us-news/michigan-father-files-1m-suit-after-teacher-cuts-his-biracial-n1279430.

CHAPTER 4

Through the Eyes of the Beholder
STIGMAS OF (DREAD) LOCS

Talé A. Mitchell

Dreadlocks, also known as *locs* or *dreads*, are ropelike strands of hair formed by matting, braiding, or twisting it in its natural form.[1] Some believe that the first recorded images of dreadlocks are in illustrations of the writing system used in Ancient Egypt, hieroglyphics, and mummies of Pharaohs and Egyptian Kings, such as Tutankhamun.[2] However, before Ancient Egypt, dreadlocks were referenced in the Hindu Vedic scriptures, the Bible, and in visual in Greek kouros sculptures from the archaic period.[3] They were also worn by the Queens of Poland and African warriors and during medieval times and the era of the Vikings; further, Shakespeare wrote of them in *Macbeth*.[4] They may even predate humans; some ancient animals' hair developed dreadlocks.

Some people believe dreadlocks are the result of the transatlantic slave trade. However, before slavery, Africans wore their hair in braids, cornrows, dreadlocks, and other styles representing social status, tribes, wealth, and talents. Some children, called Dada, were even born with dreadlocks.[5] During the transatlantic slave trade, European slavers cut the Africans' hair because they believed it was unsanitary, nasty, and dreadful; this act was a cruel means of stripping the Africans of their culture.[6] Others believe that the Africans' newly shaved heads grew matted hair during the two-to-three-month journey across the Atlantic. When the Africans exited the ships, the slave traders saw their unclean bodies and matted hair and labeled them "dreadful." Bert Ashe, the author of *Twisted: My Dreadlock Chronicles* believes this story is just that, a story, because the travel time was not long enough for dreadlocks to form, and, further, there is no documentation (oral histories, journals, et cetera) to support this claim.[7]

No one culture or event can indisputably claim the origin of dreadlocks. While we may never know the origin, we can agree that in the Western world they often have negative associations. Furthermore, although many different races and ethnicities have worn dreadlocks, the style is most popular in the Black culture and often undesirable in the white world. This chapter explores the aesthetic perceptions and controversial stereotypes and stigmas of locs.[8]

RASTAS AND POPULAR CULTURE

Smoking marijuana, knowing where to acquire it, and listening to reggae music are behaviors stereotypically associated with Jamaicans and Rastas with dreadlocks. Rastafarianism is a religion or religious movement and way of life developed in the 1930s in Jamaica. Rastafarians, or Rastas, follow Rastafarianism, a religious movement that demands societal liberation and the resettlement of the African Diaspora in Africa.[9]

Although not a Rastafarian himself, Jamaican-born Marcus Garvey, a Black nationalist who taught Black self-empowerment, is credited with being the founder of the Rastafari movement.[10] Jamaicans believed Garvey was a prophet because he predicted the crowning of the Black king Haile Selassie. Formally named Ras (meaning *king*) Tafari (one who is respected or feared), Makonnenwas Selassie became the emperor of Ethiopia in 1930 and reigned until 1974.[11] Jamaicans believed Selassie was Jah (God) or a reincarnation of Jesus. Rastafarians followed Selassie's ideology; Black people should return to Africa.

Like the biblical Samson, Rastas believed their hair was the strength of their mind, body, and spirit. Because they did not alter (comb or cut) their hair, it became matted, or locked. Unfortunately, their dreadlocks were perceived as dirty, disgusting, and frightening. It was said that those who wore them feared God and would live a dreadful life. This belief system is also recognized in the label *dreadlocks*.[12]

Bob Marley, a Rastafarian and a legendary Jamaican reggae artist, is credited for bringing dreadlocks to popular culture in the 1960s.[13] His music advocated for social change, and his success brought attention to his way of life and his dreadlocks. During the Black Power and Black is Beautiful movements of the 1960s, Black people began to embrace their natural hair and racial identities.[14] By the 1970s, dreadlocks were a part of popular culture, as an aesthetic hairstyle with a statement of self-acceptance.

Since the 1970s, many successful Black people have prided themselves on their dreadlocks. In popular culture: actress-comedian Whoopi Goldberg in the 1980s; singer-songwriters Lauryn Hill, Erykah Badu, and Lenny Kravitz and author Toni Morrison in the 1990s; hip-hop artists Lil Wayne and Wiz Khalifa, NFL players Devin Hester and Marshawn Lynch in the 2000s and 2010s. Those who wear them because of their culture call them *locs*, thus removing the negative historical connotation of *dreadful*.[15] For this reason, this chapter will use the word *locs* when referring to this natural hairstyle.

STIGMAS

Unfortunately, those who have locs are labeled with several negative stereotypes. They are often perceived as militant and even criminals. Some of these connotations derived from MOVE, a Black revolutionary group formed in 1972 in West Philadelphia, led by John Africa. Their radical ideology was to eliminate *the system:* police, animal brutality, pollution, technology, and anything unnatural or manufactured. However, their tactics disrupted their community. Using bullhorns at all times of the day and night, they conducted demonstrations against institutions that did not share their agenda.[16] The dominant culture considered them dreadlock-wearing criminals, barbarians, scum, aggressive, violent, and menaces to Philadelphia. In a 1978 standoff with the city police, the group shot and killed police officer James Ramp. Although only one deadly bullet hit Ramp, four women and five men were charged with murder and given sentences from thirty years to life in prison. Eight years later, when MOVE refused to vacate its base, the Philadelphia police dropped a bomb on its compound, setting it on fire and killing six adults and five children.[17]

People who wear locs are also accused of not washing their hair; thus, their locs are dirty, foul-smelling, and possibly even infested with lice or other hair bugs. Others are told locs look unprofessional and unkempt and that women who wear locs are lesbians.[18] I wanted to explore these stigmas from the perspective of those who currently or previously had locs. I spoke to seventy-five individuals. The youngest was eighteen, and the oldest sixty-seven; however, more than half were between twenty-eight and forty-seven. They self-identified as male, female, or genderqueer and Black or African American, Hispanic or Latino, and Native American or American Indian. Their education levels ranged from high school diploma to PhD. They had careers in various industries, with positions ranging from entry-level to senior executives and CEOs. Sixty-two of those surveyed said their jobs required them to interact with consumers. Their hair length varied from shorter than ear length to below the waist, but most had mid-back or shoulder-length locs, and they had grown them from less than a year to twenty-three years.

HOW IT ALL BEGAN

I began by asking how and why they grew their locs. Thirty-one said that they started them as comb coils: "a neatly spiraled curl done to the hair by use of a rat tail comb."[19] The two-strand twist, in which two small sections of hair are twisted together, was the second most common way. Other methods were braids or plaits, backcombing, interlocking or sisterlocking, adding loc extensions or yarn, letting locs form organically (washed but never detangled), and palm-rolling. Backcombing uses a comb to matt the hair, and interlock or sisterlock uses a latch hook to loop the hair into a loc. In loc extensions, extra hair (usually synthetic) wraps the original strand of hair, and yarn is a wrapping technique that takes a strand of the original hair and wraps it with yarn. Organic, or freeform, locs are not manipulated into twists; the hair is just left to form as it will (these are the locs worn by Rastafari culture). Finally, palm-rolled locs start when stylists roll individual sections of hair between their hands to create a coil.

The people I interviewed grew their locs for various reasons: fashion trends, connections to their African roots, aesthetics, rebelling against the norm, religion, culture, and other outside influences, I identified eight themes among these responses. First, locs are low maintenance: "People I knew with kinkier hair said they loved the low maintenance." "It's best for my hair. I don't have to do too much to start my day." Unfortunately, the benefit of low maintenance hair is directly connected to the stigmas that locs are disgusting because those with locs do not wash their hair.

The next theme was a combination of growth, health, and a wish to have natural and authentic hair. Many believed that having natural locs free of chemicals and heat would allow their hair healthy growth. Locs are also a symbol of authenticity: "It was my commitment to myself to be authentically me for life," and "I wanted to be natural and connect to the most authentic me."

Others talked a lot about culture and ancestry. Locs represented their culture and connected them to their ancestors: "I continued having dreams about my hair growing and believe it is ancestral," and "I was embracing my culture, and it was before they [locs] were trending."

Culture and ancestry can be linked to another common theme: spirituality. During slavery, white slaveowners forced their Christian religion on enslaved Africans. At the same time, enslaved Africans gathered together and practiced their native rituals, danced, told stories, and sang songs as a way to connect to their spirituality.[20] One respondent explained, "I believe that my crown is my glory. Crown meaning head. Locs to me is a spiritual walk, and it takes dedication and commitment to God." Another simply stated that "spiritual growth and awakening" were the reason for their locs.

Others wanted to create new beginnings. One individual wanted to reinvent themselves when they went away to college. Some just wanted a new look to mark a life change: "I was going thru a transition in life. I wanted to walk into my new lifestyle with no toxins in my body." We get bored with our lives and want changes and new challenges, leaving our baggage behind and becoming a better version of ourselves. Extreme changes to our hair, like cutting it or going natural, can represent reinvention or transformation.[21]

Similarly, rebellion surfaced as a theme. Sometimes people rebel because they believe someone or something has challenged their human rights. All humans have the right to their opinions and deserve to be treated with respect. One individual said she rebelled to express how she felt about how society treats Black women. "I felt like I wanted to be different from what society makes us as Black women feel like we have to look." Another individual shared the experience that caused her to rebel: "I had an experience at work where a white woman made my hair the topic of a teaching evaluation. At that time, I was wearing a wig. I decided that respectability politics gets us nowhere as melanated people. If they wanted to spend time in a professional space talking about my hair, we could talk about locs next."

The most popular reason people grew their locs was that they were influenced by popular culture or someone they knew. "Chris Rock's documentary *Good Hair* pushed the envelope. . . . Seeing that the industry was making a goldmine out of Black women trying to adhere to European beauty standards all while cutting them out of having a seat at the table disturbed me to my core."

PERCEPTIONS OF ME

These responses led me to ask participants if they thought their locs played a role in how people perceived them. Thirty-three of the seventy-five said it didn't, but forty-one said yes, it definitely changed the way people perceive them. One person that proudly described themselves as "Black, queer, and fat" said white people were taught that locs are dirty. They wondered how the white people they worked with really felt about them. White people often think they are Jamaican, and some ask them what island they were from, as if they were from another planet. Supporting militant and criminal stigmas, one also expressed how appalled they were when their white boss told them that their hair made them look scary. Yet not just white people perceive people differently because of their locs. A few said Black people often ask them why they wanted to wear their hair "like that," and some notice that other Black people treat them differently than they do Black people without locs.

I wanted to know if they experienced other common stigmas as well. Many of the stereotypes echoed the ones already discussed, but they added a more profound meaning. As expected, they most often deal with others assuming they smoke or sell marijuana or are Rasta and do not wash their hair. The second most common stigmas were that they listen to reggae music, they are militant, and the women are lesbians. Some other stigmas included being criminals, uneducated, lazy, unemployed, thugs, or football players. The least mentioned stigma was that locs have lice or other hair bugs. Most believe that stigmas result from what is portrayed as beautiful in the media, and we as a county are very judgmental, and our society is highly Europeanized.[22]

PROFESSIONALISM

I probed further and asked about professionalism. Many said their families expressed that locs were unprofessional and were concerned they would result in fewer job opportunities or that employers would not take them seriously. One respondent said their mom thought locs were inappropriate for a corporate setting and suggested they should have "long, neat, and straight hair." A senior member of one respondent's family stated, "In my generation, dreadlocks were associated with being unkempt, and I do not think that has changed." Their families intended to "look out for family"; however, they too are influenced by the media and often show ignorance about locs.

This opinion was also expressed in employment and educational settings. One respondent said that the human resources department in their workplace declared: "It's not professional, and that is it." Another was told the same at a job interview with a white man, and another heard it from a professor. A coworker was trying to be "helpful" by telling one participant that the military thinks locs are unprofessional. Another expressed that the negative comments came not from a colleague or administration but from a security guard.

Respondents were asked if they would cut their hair at the request of a current or prospective employer. Although about half of them had cut their locs in the past, almost all, seventy-two out of seventy-five, would not cut their locs if their employer asked them, and sixty-eight would not cut their locs to get a job. The few who said they would cut them would do so to provide for their families where absolutely necessary, maintain their financial independence, or receive a significant pay increase. Nevertheless, in each case, an individual is forced to choose between financially providing for their families and keeping their hair.

SOCIAL POLI-TRICKS AND LEGISLATION

In America, Title VII prohibits employment discrimination based on race, color, religion, sex, and national origin.[23] The act has been amended to include, among other concerns, sexual harassment, gender identity, and sexual orientation. However, in most states, discrimination based on hairstyle is not protected under Title VII.[24]

To determine whether respondents were aware of these laws and highly publicized incidents of discrimination, they were presented with summaries of six incidences of discrimination against individuals wearing locs. More than half of the participants were unaware of each occurrence.

Racial Profiling

In 2013, seven-year-old Tiana Parker of Tulsa, Oklahoma, was sent home because Deborah Brown Community Charter School officials insisted her locs were "not presentable and distracted from the respectful and serious atmosphere [the school] strives for." Parker's parents were rightfully outraged. The school directed the Parkers to its dress code: "Hairstyles such as locs, afros, mohawks, and other faddish styles are unacceptable." Parker's parents refused to cut Tiana's locs and remove her from the school. There was a substantial public backlash, and soon afterward, the school changed its policy to allow such hairstyles.[25]

Only twenty-nine of the study participants were aware of this circumstance. Their reactions suggested this was a case of *racial profiling*—according to *Merriam-Webster,* "discrimination against minorities based on stereotypes." It is entirely inappropriate group locs and Afros with mohawks and define them as faddish styles. Tiana's mother stated, "Afros are how one's hair naturally grows, and locs are very similar to that, so I think it is extremely offensive, and that policy targets a specific population." Tiana was ostracized for her hair, yet her school had no policies relating to unnatural hairstyles like mohawks with wild hair colors.

Social Pressure

The second incident involved sixteen-year-old Tyler House of Markham, Illinois (a Chicago suburb), who was fired from her job at Marcus Cinema in

2016 for having locs. "Their decision was based on ignorance of the culture and history of locs." Marcus Cinema stated that its grooming policy disallowing locs was an old one and promised to update it by removing the ban on locs. Although Marcus Cinema changed its policy, Tyler's mother, Darnetta Herring, believed the company did so only because of the negative publicity.

Considerably fewer respondents, only eleven, were aware of Tyler House's case. *Social pressure* was the overall theme of their responses. Respondents overwhelmingly agreed with Darnetta Herring: "They only backtracked to avoid being cast as discriminatory."

Microaggressions

In the same year, 2016, Rachel Sakabo accused St. Regis, a luxury hotel in Manhattan, New York, of firing her as a front-desk concierge because she had locs. Her manager pointed out the establishment's policy of not allowing braids at the front desk. "They aren't braids; they're locs," Sakabo explained, but the manager replied, "Well, can you unlock them?" Consequently, the hotel fired Sakabo—not because of her locs (according to the hotel) but because she "wasn't a good fit with the culture of the establishment." The management then recommended her for a "better fit" hotel owned by the same company (Marriott Inc.), the W hotel. The W hotels are trendy, not as upscale, and more laid back, and their guests tend to be younger.[26]

Only nine respondents were familiar with this case; however, all of them agreed that this was a microaggression. While the stated reasons for her termination were rather ambiguous, respondents agreed her hair was the true reason. A few pointed out several racial microaggressions just in the summary of the incident. "Can you unlock them? You are not a good fit with this establishment's culture, and you would better fit in at a hotel that is not so upscale." What culture are they referring to? Although Rachel was qualified for the job, St. Regis did not want her to be its public face. In asking her to "unlock" her hair, the hotel "expected her to conform not just in appearance but cultural conformity, and that is extremely biased and offensive."

The Power of Social Media

Savion J. Wright of Austin, Texas, amazed an interviewer with the required skills for the job; however, the interviewer asked, "Would you mind cutting your hair? We would like our partners to be professional, and I don't think your look would fly well. . . . So, just consider it." Wright turned down the job and immediately went to Facebook to share his experience. His story went viral, with sixteen thousand responses and ten thousand shares.[27]

I was surprised that only eleven participants were aware of this case. Nevertheless, most believed he did the right thing by turning down the job, and they were proud of him. Many expressed admiration because he posted it on social media for the world to see. "He did right and turned down the position. I'm happy more awareness is being brought to establishments with this wayward thought pattern and policies in place." However, not everyone has the luxury of turning down a job.

Stand Your Ground

A highly publicized and often cited case of natural hair discrimination occurred in 2010 when Catastrophe Management Solutions (CMS) withdrew its job offer to the qualified Chastity Jones because she would not cut her locs. The hiring manager attempted to justify the decision: "They tend to get messy." CMS's grooming policy stated that its employees must have a "presentable image," and it banned "excessive hairstyles."[28]

This case became a civil rights issue and was taken to court. Now, it is the benchmark of an incident that exposed racial discrimination in the workplace because of natural Black hairstyles. Thus the for this occurrence is theme as *stand your ground*. The Equal Employment Opportunity Commission (EEOC) filed a racial discrimination lawsuit against CMS on Jones's behalf. The EEOC argued that CMS used negative racial stereotypes that suggest natural Black hair is unprofessional and unpresentable in the workplace. Both a federal court, in 2014, and a federal court of appeals, in 2016 ruled in favor of CMS. The courts stated: "Hairstyles, even one more closely associated with a particular ethnic group," are not fixed characteristics [immutable] but a hairstyle of choice [mutable] for a Black person and therefore, is not discrimination nor protected under Title VII."[29] In other words, employers have the legal right to ban employees from having locs in the workplace. In fact, in 2018, the US Supreme Court refused even to review Jones's case.

Criminal and Humiliating

Finally, fifty-two of the seventy-five were aware of one of the most publicized occurrences of hair discrimination that inspired change. Alan Maloney, a referee at Buena Regional High School in Buena, New Jersey, directed a referee, Alan Maloney, to cut off the locs of sixteen-year-old high school wrestler Andrew Johnson. He did so in front of spectators just as he went out on the floor for his match. A video of the incident went viral when New Jersey sportscaster Mike Frankel posted it to his Twitter account.[30] According to CNN, the NFHS rule book states: "A wrestler's hair cannot fall below the top of a shirt collar in the back, below his earlobes on the sides, or below his eyebrows. If it is longer than the rule allows, the wrestler has to braid his hair or hide it beneath a hair cover attached to his ear guards."[31] Johnson's hair was covered, yet Maloney insisted that Johnson cut his locs or forfeit his match.[32] Faced with adversity, Johnson went on to win the match.

This occurrence was given the themes *criminal* and *humiliating*. The referee and trainer assaulted Andrew, and criminal charges should have been filed. One respondent even called it assault with a deadly weapon. It was clear that Andrew was humiliated. It happened publicly in an auditorium where the focus was explicitly on the wrestlers.

These circumstances refer specifically to loc hairstyles; however, many other Black hairstyles—including Afros, braids, cornrows, Bantu knots, and twists—have also been discriminated against.[33]

Change Is Gonna Come

On July 3, 2019, California's governor, Gavin Newsom, signed a bill banning workplaces and schools from discriminating against Black people for wearing natural hairstyles, including locs, braids, twists, Afros, and cornrows. Senator Holly Mitchell, also of California, authored and proposed the CROWN Act: "Create a Respectful and Open Workplace for Natural Hair." Mitchell had already been working on the act, but the Andrew Johnson case inspired her to push forward. California became the first state to sign into law a bill protecting Black people from being discriminated against because of their natural hair.[34] Later that month, New York followed suit by amending its Human Rights Law and its Dignity for All Students Act. New York's Governor Andrew Cuomo signed the bill that added "traits historically associated with race, including, but not limited to, hair texture and protective hairstyles" to the definition of race. The incident of the teenage wrestler, Andrew Johnson, inspired both Bills.[35] As of July 2022, eighteen out of forty-two states with the act on their dockets had passed the CROWN Act. New Jersey (inspired by the Andrew Johnson story), Connecticut, Maryland, Virginia (the first southern state), Colorado, and Washington.[36]

Locs are clearly not just a contemporary hairstyle but a cultural phenomenon that has led to political, legal, and professional disputes.[37] To date, scholarly dialogue on the topic of natural Black hair has encompassed a variety of natural hairstyles—like Afros, cornrows, braids—and primarily focuses on Black women's natural hair.[38] This dialogue differs because it specifically focuses on locs. This discourse considers the countless instances in which Black people with locs have faced discrimination and scrutiny in public areas, professional settings, academic institutions, and courtrooms. It is essential to educate people and remove negative connotations associated with locs. With more states adopting the CROWN Act, I am optimistic that change is on the horizon.

NOTES

1. Ayana D. Byrd and Lori L. Tharps, *Hair Story: Untangling the Roots of Black Hair in America*, 2nd ed. (New York: St. Martin's, 2014).
2. Jennifer Hruby, "Hieroglyphics," *Keywords Glossary*, Theories of Media, Univ. of Chicago, Winter 2003, https://csmt.uchicago.edu/glossary2004/hieroglyphics.htm; Taylor Bryant, "The Fascinating History of Locs," *Refinery29*, Dec. 20, 2017, https://www.refinery29.com/en-us/2015/04/86174/history-of-dreadlocks.
3. Bert Ashe, *Twisted: My Dreadlock Chronicles* (Evanston, IL: Agate Bolden, 2015).
4. Pumza Fihlani, "South Africa's Dreadlock Thieves," *BBC News*, Feb. 27, 2013, https://www.bbc.com/news/world-africa-21498878; Kevin Frank, "Whether Beast or Human: The Cultural Legacies of Dread, Locks, and Dystopia," *CUNY Academic Works* (2007): 18, https://academicworks.cuny.edu/cgi/viewcontent.cgi?article=1185&context=bb_pubs.
5. Kira Byrd, "How to Get Dreadlocks: Origin, History, Hairstyles, and More," *Curl Centric*, May 8, 2018, https://www.curlcentric.com/dreadlocks/.
6. Byrd and Tharps, *Hair Story*.
7. Ashe, *Twisted*; Rumeana Jahangir, "How Does Black Hair Reflect Black History?," *BBC News*, May 31, 2015, https://www.bbc.com/news/uk-england-merseyside-31438273.
8. Ayana D. Byrd and Lori L. Tharps, "When Black Hair Is Against the Rules," *New York Times*, May 1, 2014.
9. M. Kuumba and Femi Ajanaku, "Dreadlocks: The Hair Aesthetics of Cultural Resistance and Collective Identity Formation," *Mobilization: An International Quarterly* 3 (Oct. 1, 1998): 227–43.
10. Tony Martin, "Religions—Rastafari: Marcus Garvey," *BBC News*, last updated Oct. 21, 2009, http://www.bbc.co.uk/religion/religions/rastafari/people/marcusgarvey.shtml.
11. Maboula Soumahoro, "From Garvey to Marley: Rastafari Theology Noel Leo Erskine," *Souls* 9 (Aug. 27, 2007): 272–73.
12. Jessica Clover, "A Short History of Dreadlocks, the Prehistoric Hairstyle," *A Jamaica Experience*, Dec. 29, 2018, www.ajamaicaexperience.com/history-of-dreadlocks/.
13. James A. Winders, "Reggae, Rastafarians and Revolution: Rock Music in the Third World," *Journal of Popular Culture* 17 (Summer 1983): 61–73.
14. Stephanie M. H. Camp, "Black Is Beautiful: An American History," *Journal of Southern History* 81 (Aug. 2015): 675–90.
15. Del Sandeen, "A Brief Look into Locs (or Locks) for Black Hair," *Byrdit*, updated on Mar. 20, 2022, https://www.byrdie.com/locs-or-locks-400267.
16. Anna Orso, "MOVE 101: Why, 34 Years Ago, Philadelphia Dropped a Bomb on Itself," *Billy Penn*, May 13, 2019, https://billypenn.com/2019/05/13/move-101-why-30-years-ago-philadelphia-dropped-a-bomb-on-itself/.

17. Ed Pilkington, "A Siege. A Bomb. 48 Dogs. And the Black Commune That Would Not Surrender," *Guardian,* July 31, 2018, https://www.theguardian.com/world/2018/jul/31/a-siege-a-bomb-48-dogs-and-the-black-commune-that-would-not-surrender.

18. Victoria Uwumarogie, "Don't Be like Giuliana Rancic: 11 Assumptions People Make about Those Who Wear Locs That Don't Make Sense," *MadameNoire,* Feb. 25, 2015, https://madamenoire.com/514036/dont-like-giuliana-rancic-assumptions-people-locs-dont-make-sense/.

19. "Comb Coils for the Straightforward Dreadlocks Solution," *Majestic Locs* (blog), https://majesticlocs.com/comb-coils/, site discontinued as of Sept. 26, 2022.

20. Mark Leone, "The Problem: Religion within the World of Slaves," *Current Anthropology* 61, no. S22 (2020): 276–88.

21. Lisa Marie Bobby, "How to Reinvent Yourself," *Growing Self* (blog), Aug. 2, 2021, https://www.growingself.com/reinvent-yourself/.

22. Talé A. Mitchell, "CRT and Colorism: A Manifestation of Whitewashing in Marketing Communication?," *Journal of Marketing Management* 36, no. 11 (Sept. 2020), https://doi.org/10.1080/0267257X.2020.1794934.

23. "Title VII of the Civil Rights Act of 1964," Pub. L. No. 88–352, § 2000e, available at Equal Employment Opportunity Commission website, accessed Aug. 1, 2019, https://www.eeoc.gov/laws/statutes/titlevii.cfm.

24. Arthur B. Smith Jr., Charles B. Craver, and Ronald Turner, *Employment Discrimination Law: Cases and Materials,* 7th ed. (Durham, NC: Carolina Academic Press, 2011).

25. Andrea Eger, "Parents Outraged after Daughter's Hairstyle Not Allowed at Deborah Brown Community School," *Tulsa World News,* Sept. 8, 2013; #TeamEBONY, "Tiana Parker's Old School Changes Policy on Afros, Dreads," *EBONY,* Sept. 10, 2013, https://www.ebony.com/tiana-parkers-old-school-changes-policy-on-afros-dreads-981/.

26. Talal Ansari and Salvador Hernandez, "This Woman Says She Was Fired from an Upscale Hotel over Her Dreadlocks," *BuzzFeed News,* July 29, 2016, www.buzzfeednews.com/article/talalansari/st-regis-braids.

27. Savion J. Wright, "I Went to a Job Interview. It Went Extremely," Facebook, Sept. 24, 2016, https://www.facebook.com/thesavionwright/posts/1333503336659828.

28. Noel Gutierrez-Morfin, "U. S. Court Rules Dreadlock Ban during Hiring Process Is Legal," *NBC News,* Sept. 21, 2016.

29. Taryn Finley, "Appeals Court Rules Employers Can Ban Dreadlocks at Work," *HuffPost,* Sept. 20, 2016, https://www.huffingtonpost.com/entry/appeals-court-rules-dreadlocks-work_us_57e0252ae4b0071a6e08a7c3.

30. Mike Frankel (@MikeFrankelJSZ), "Epitome of a Team Player," *Twitter,* 12:54 P.M., Dec. 20, 2018, https://twitter.com/mikefrankeljsz/status/1075811774954463235.

31. Amir Vera, "Family of the Black Wrestler Who Was Forced to Cut His Dreadlocks Speaks Out," *CNN Online,* Dec. 26, 2018, https://www.cnn.com/2018/12/25/us/wrestler-dreadlocks-new-jersey-comments/index.html.

32. Associated Press, "Olympian Reaches out to Wrestler Forced to Cut Dreadlocks, Slams Ref's Decision," *Los Angeles Times,* Dec. 22, 2018.

33. Smith, Craver, and Turner, *Employment Discrimination Law.*

34. Phil Willon and Alexa Diaz, "California Becomes First State to Ban Discrimination Based on One's Natural Hair," *Los Angeles Times*, July 3, 2019.

35. Andrew Cuomo, "Governor Cuomo Signs S6209a/A7797a to Make Clear Civil Rights Laws Ban Discrimination against Hair Styles or Textures Associated with Race," July 12, 2019, https://www.govinfo.gov/content/pkg/CRPT-116hrpt525/html/CRPT-116hrpt525-pt1.htm; Janelle Griffith, "New York Is Second State to Ban Discrimination Based on Natural Hairstyles," *NBC News*, July 15, 2019, https://www.nbcnews.com/news/nbcblk/new-york-second-state-ban-discrimination-based-natural-hairstyles-n1029931.

36. Leah Rodriguez, "8 States Across the US That Have Banned Black Hair Discrimination," *Global Citizen: Demand Equality,* Mar. 2, 2021, www.globalcitizen.org/en/content/hair-discrimination-crown-act-states/.

37. EEOC v. Catastrophic Management Solutions, No. 2016 WL 4916851 (US Court of Appeals for the 11th Circuit Sept. 16, 2016); Finley, "Appeals Court Rules Employers Can Ban Dreadlocks at Work."

38. Ingrid Banks, *Hair Matters: Beauty, Power, and Black Women's Consciousness* (New York: New York Univ. Press, 2000); Tameka N. Ellington, "Social Networking Sites: A Support System for African-American Women Wearing Natural Hair," *International Journal of Fashion Design, Technology and Education* 8 (2015): 21–29; Shirley Tate, "Black Beauty: Shade, Hair and Anti-Racist Aesthetics," *Ethnic and Racial Studies* 30 (Mar. 1, 2007): 300–319; Cheryl Thompson, "Black Women, Beauty, and Hair as a Matter of Being," *Women's Studies* 38 (Oct. 15, 2009): 831–56; H. Shellae Versey, "Centering Perspectives on Black Women, Hair Politics, and Physical Activity," *American Journal of Public Health* 104 (May 2014): 810–15.

CHAPTER 5

I'm Free Now!

THE SELF-ESTEEM AND SELF-SCHEMA OF AFRICAN AMERICAN WOMEN WEARING NATURAL HAIR

Tameka N. Ellington

A woman's hairstyle expresses much about her identity; specifically, hair texture is one of the most visible signifiers of racial identity.[1] The hair texture of African American women tells a story of life's advantages and hardships. African American hair valuations are rooted in slavery and White supremacy, and historically, hair valuations have been discouraging for African American women because they are rated based on the White standard of beauty, which dictates that anything other than White is unattractive.[2] Socially, beauty is an objective and universal embodiment that often values the unrealistic, in this case, it demands that African American women must mimic their White counterparts to be considered attractive. In this way, according to Naomi Wolf, beauty becomes a means of controlling individuals to fit a certain mold that the "privileged" few have established. Western, specifically North American, values of beauty are defined as Whiteness, youth, thinness, wealth, symmetry, and lack of disability. With any deviation, one becomes less attractive.[3]

Today, after hundreds of years of being told that African features are unattractive, or "bad," African American women face the societal truth that their hair texture, be it "good" or "bad," has the power to dictate their social and possibly their economic fate.[4] As a result, many African American women's level of self-esteem, one's view of their worth and self-schema, one's belief system based on long-lasting memories and life experiences, regarding their hair suffers.[5]

This ideology of "good" and "bad" hair continues to work against African American women and girls because their naturally kinky hair texture is reduced to being unattractive. More specifically, the unspoken cultural divide among African American women is dictated by the type of lifestyle certain hair textures provides them. Those born with straighter hair and, to some degree, even those who straighten their hair chemically receive more privileges than those who wear their naturally kinky hair.[6] *Natural hair* refers to the hair of those of African descent or peoples of the African Diaspora that has not been straightened or altered by chemical products. Natural hair is not fully accepted among the mainstream society or within the African American community.[7]

The term *pressed* or *straightened* means that one has used heat and a metal comb to straighten natural hair. A perm or relaxer is a creamy chemical product used to straighten natural hair. Based on the dominant Western or European standards, straight hair is considered the most beautiful: "Hair straightening is not only linked to physical attractiveness, but it is also a marker of socio-economic mobility."[8] Those with straight hair remain privileged to join certain organizations, have higher-paying jobs, and partner with a "higher" caliber of man than those wearing kinky hair. In 2013, Melphine Evans, an African American female ex-executive of BP Oil, was fired because she started wearing her natural hair.[9] This is one example of many discriminatory situations where African American women's quality of life suffered because their kinky hair texture was deemed unacceptable by the dominant society.

The African American community, via bigoted conditioning, also buys into the concepts of "good" and "bad" hair by believing that *beauty* is synonymous with and contingent on having straight hair. Straightening the hair is the default for African American women because of the "tenacious [societal] hold" on the African American community regarding the lack of beauty associated with African features.[10] Research shows that most African American men prefer their female counterparts with straight hair instead of the kinky hair they were born with.[11] Black hair researcher Cheryl Thompson has hypothesized that the issue is the lack of self-history.[12] Fellow Black hair researcher Brina Hargo notes that modern African American women justify straightening their hair by explaining that they are not trying to conform to a Caucasian beauty standard but that they find their natural hair texture too foreign, as they have not worn it its original texture since childhood. Or they may believe it unmanageable, undesirable to the opposite sex or a potential employer, or just ugly.[13]

Falling in line with mainstream ideology, "Hair alteration is the default aesthetic process for African American women"; however, since the beginning of the natural hair movement in the early 2000s, African American women have been redefining what beauty is, via a "counter-hegemonic strategy."[14] Some women wear natural hair (referred to as "going natural") and in the process are becoming more educated about themselves and the overall African American culture because they have to "learn their hair." This newfound "authentic Black beauty" can result in a feeling of being "free," because wearing straightened hair has been known to be restrictive and hazardous in the lives of African American women.[15] African American women wearing straightened hair incur a financial burden to maintain it, physical effects from burns and lesions on the scalp, and a lack of exercise resulting from an attempt to preserve the straight hairstyle.

Thus, the main objective of this research was to evaluate the self-esteem and self-schema of African American women wearing natural hair. The goal was to understand how the White standard of beauty has shaped the women's life experiences and influenced their cognitive and behavioral selves regarding their hair and to determine whether there had been a shift in the perceptions of Black hair over nine years. The results indicate minor shifts; however, the overall message about Black hair remains the same. The need for legislation signed in 2019 to protect Blacks against hair discrimination validates that society still has issues with Black hair.[16] Further, a 2020 *HuffPost* article suggests that Black women still have negative feelings about their hair.[17]

Hence, the author asked these questions while collating data: Have respondents had life experiences that have countered their thoughts on the White standard of beauty? If so, how have these experiences influenced their appearance self-schema regarding their natural hair? What is the level of self-esteem African American women have of themselves and their natural hair? In what ways have their life experiences influenced their self-esteem about their hair? Did African American women change their overall perception of natural hair between 2003 and 2012?

METHODS

The current research evaluates the experiences of African American women and is a continuation of a 2003 study.[18] The author compared those earlier responses with those in 2012 to evaluate if an enhancement in the perceptions of natural hair occurred. All participants were recruited through a snowball sampling process, and they were given pseudonyms to protect their privacy. The median age was 47.65 years. The length of time the participants wore natural hair varied from just one week to twenty-four years. In 2003, the majority of participants (72 percent) wore locs, and in 2012, they wore a variety of different hairstyles, from an Afro one day to a two-strand twist and then braids the next day. Sixty-eight percent of participants in this second sample talked about how being natural is "trendy" now. This phenomenon was theorized as the rationale for the greater variety of styles worn. Also, during the interviewing process, the participants completed the "Perceptions of African Americans on their Natural Hair" questionnaire, including the Rosenberg Self-Esteem Scale in the first section.[19] The second section of the questionnaire evaluated the participants' level of hair texture acceptance. The interviewing guide and questionnaire were updated for the latter participants based on a recent review of the literature and the recent variety in the hairstyles worn. The responses were analyzed for themes and patterns.

RESULTS

Four themes emerged from the data: first, childhood and other experiences with the good and bad hair concept; second, dealing with unsupportive family members and others; third, level of self-esteem and self-schema based on life experiences, and fourth, quality of life enhancement after wearing natural hair.

Past Experiences with Good and Bad Hair

In a study I conducted evaluating the virtual natural hair movement, one of the participants profoundly stated, "African Americans are the only race who can look at their offspring's hair in disdain and talk negatively about it." This unfortunate declaration was in line with the data that emerged in the current study. Many participants in the 2012 study reflected on their childhood and their negative experiences regarding their hair. In younger years, all participants were schematic on the White standard of beauty; that is, they were extremely concerned with wanting to be accepted within the overall society. Their parents also wanted their daughters to be accepted and fit in. Carla (2012) recalled a time in the late 1970s when she was in the seventh grade, and her mother bought her a wiglet to conceal or enhance her "super short" hair. "It was horrible for me. . . . I went to a sleepover, and the girls would try to knock it off. . . . The entire night I was trying to keep my wiglet on my head." "Super short" hair is considered "bad" hair in the African American community. The White standard of beauty has programmed many African Americans to believe they must also have long, flowing hair—"good" hair—to be beautiful. Achieving this standard without straightening or perming the hair and adding weave is impossible because of the vast difference in the hair textures of people of African descent and Whites. The term *weave* refers to human or synthetic hair extensions applied to the permed/relaxed hair to add length and fullness. In an attempt to transform their daughters' kinky, "bad" hair to straighter "good" hair, mothers would use hot metal combs to press their daughters' hair, even when the girls were as young as three years old. Caerla also remembers that her mom once accidentally dropped a hot straightening comb down her back and burned her. The dire measures to live up to the standard caused harm to many participants, who discussed getting burns on their scalps, ears, and necks.

Participants in both samples believed good versus bad hair is an ignorant concept resulting from racial degradation engrained from slavery times. The phenomenon remains a dogma that stifles many during crucial self-esteem development. "I fell victim to this; I thought I had bad hair," Elaine (2012) confessed. Falling victim meant this participant believed her hair was not beautiful because of its kinky nature and deemed it inappropriate to wear her natural hair. On a lighter note, Stephanie (2012) could now find humor in the societal concept that had previously plagued her life when she stated, "Bad hair is hair that attacks you. Has my hair ever attacked anybody?" This response suggested that the participant has positively evolved, leaving the negative White beauty standard behind her, even if others are unwilling to join her on her journey. The word *journey* here refers to someone's experiences going natural and maintaining natural hair. The author of this chapter is an African American woman who wears natural hair and is a heuristic researcher, having a hair journey similar to the participants'.

Unsupportive Family and Others

As stated earlier, African American women have faced nonacceptance of their natural hair from mainstream society, the African American community, and even their family members. The data revealed that many participants could not depend on family and friends for support after deciding to wear natural hair. The participants' responses suggested that family and others were continually schematic on the White standard of beauty and were very concerned about the participants fitting into this standard. Sixty-eight percent stated that their family and others do accepting their natural hair, and as a result, many have faced interracial and intraracial microaggressive behaviors and statements. Carla's mother told her, "If you want to live in Africa, you can just go back." Her mother believed that by wearing natural hair, her daughter looked *too* closely connected to her African slave roots. Historically, the members of the African American community have believed that admitting their connection with Africa somehow degraded their level of education, social status, and beauty. Therefore, wearing one's hair naturally was even worse than having a dark complexion. Brenda and Barbara (2012), a pair of sisters, responded similarly. "After we went natural, our mother did not speak to us for almost a month." Unsupportive families also included extended family and significant others. Iman (2003) stated that her grandparents "told me I looked like a pickaninny." *Pickaninny* is a slur for a Black child with nappy hair, often associated with characters such as Buckwheat from the 1930s television show *Little Rascals*, who is an iteration of the racist Black Sambo character created to entertain White audiences.

Eboni (2003) revealed, "My husband doesn't like [my hair]." Research published in 2018 discusses how this phenomenon is still happening.[20] Many African American men are still pressuring the women in their lives to straighten their hair. Afiya Mbilishaka's research has revealed that only 28.6 percent gave encouraging words about their female partners' wearing natural hair. Data released regarding dating apps shows that African American women are the least selected, even by African American men.[21] The data is also in line with other publications, such as BET's article "See How Black Women Are Dealing with Being Rejected by Black Men."[22] The unfortunate truth is that the Black community is still suffering from colonial mentality regarding beauty and many other aspects of the culture. Beyond family and intimate partners, nonacceptance and lack of support for Black women wearing their hair naturally has emerged in other social realms.

Regarding the economics of natural hair, some participants (16 percent in 2003 and 33 percent in 2012) explained that they believe that by wearing natural hair, they have been held back from career growth. Khadijah (2003) stated, "My boss was told that my [natural] hair was intimidating to White men and women." Carla (2012) said, "This lady told me that she likes my hair, but she can't go natural because she is a professional," insinuating that natural hair is less than professional. Many instances of discrimination at work or school have occurred in the last decade; however, these are just the ones that have obtained media attention. In 2019, in an attempt to combat the continued discrimination Blacks faced regarding their hair, California (Creating a Respectable and Open World for Naturals (the CROWN Act) and New York (New York State Human Rights Law (NYSHRL) became the first states to pass banning corporations, institutions, and so forth, from discriminating against a Black person because of their hair.

Stereotypes associated with having natural hair also emerged during the interviewing process. Saja (2012), wearing locs, stated, "I was mistaken for being Rastafarian." As explained in the literature, the femininity of African American women wearing natural hair is often questioned.[23] Natalie (2012), wearing a close-cut hairstyle, said, "Other females assumed I was gay." "I didn't think I would be sexy anymore without my long blond hair," stated Barbara (2012), who was once known for her luxurious, permed, chemically colored blond hair. Abba (2003) claimed, "It's mostly conservative Black and White people who don't like my natural hair." This comment suggests the stereotype that natural hair is for super liberal, earth-loving people. Martha (2012) continued, "One [Black] man told me, 'A woman's hair is her crown and glory, and you got some awful short glory!'" Again, the comment reinforces the stereotype that natural hair is not feminine. While enduring all of the negative experiences and lack of support, the participants proclaimed that their resiliency prevailed.

On September 21, 2018, Netflix released *Nappily Ever After,* an American romantic comedy starring Sanaa Lathan as Violet. Violet's story is centered on her seemingly perfect life—a remarkable career, a fiancé who is a doctor, and hair that is long, straight, and perfectly pressed. Her mother, Paulette, played by Lynn Whitfield, stresses that Violet must maintain her perfect hair to keep her perfect life. During the movie, Violet discovers that her fiancé is cheating on her; she returns home furious and shaves her head, thereby getting rid of the entity that had a destructive hold on her life. For African American women, maintaining straight hair is a painful and stressful experience because of the scalp burns and alopecia associated with the hair-straightening chemicals. Violet begins to look deeper inside herself to find her life's purpose, part of which is wearing her hair in its natural state.[24] This film, although fictional, was inspired by real-life stories of thousands of women of African descent—proof that there is a continued need for women to have social support to wear hair that does not adhere to White standards of beauty.

Self-Esteem/Self-Schema

As a result of wearing natural hair, participants became aschematic regarding the White standard of beauty; assimilating to this standard became irrelevant for them. The data revealed that their life experiences and memories left a lasting impression, although harsh at times. This schema developed into confidence, giving the participants the strength to reject the White ideology of beauty. After the 2003 data was analyzed, the author discovered that the majority (68 percent) of the women had high self-esteem. Thus, during the 2012 study, the author asked if it was necessary to have a certain level of self-esteem to wear natural hair: 85 percent had high self-esteem, and 83 percent believed that, because of the societal backlash, women needed high self-esteem to wear natural hair.

To understand another dimension of the participants' self-schema and self-esteem regarding their hair, "The Perceptions of African Americans on their Natural Hair" questionnaire included a section about hair texture acceptance. Of the 2003 sample, 80 percent preferred their natural hair over previous permed/relaxed hair, and of the 2012 sample, 90 percent did. When asked, "How would you describe the way you wear your hair?" 84 percent in 2003 and 85 percent in 2012 responded that their natural hair was a means of self-acceptance. During the interviewing process, Lisa (2012) admitted, "Coming to grips with yourself [and hair texture] is a brave decision." Questions were asked regarding participants' thoughts on the terminology used to describe African American textured hair (*kinky, curly, coarse, wooly, nappy,* and *wavy*). The data revealed that in both samples, *nappy* hair the worst word one could use to describe African American hair, because of its negative historical context. According to the participants, *nappy* was a term devised by slave traders/masters to describe African hair texture. The true origin of the word is complex and hard to follow; however, via the natural hair movement, which began in the early 2000s, it is being redefined within the African American community to be a positive reflection of Black culture. Websites such as Nappturality.com promote self-acceptance and provide education about caring for African American hair textures. In the process of becoming more accepting of themselves via their natural hair, they further negated White beauty standards after realizing how prohibiting their previous straight hair was to their lives physically, personally, and monetarily.

Quality of Life

In the 2003 study, the terms *afraid* and *scared* emerged in the data regarding how participants felt about their hair. So, researchers asked the 2012 participants if they were ever afraid of what their natural hair texture would look like. Of the participants, 58 percent of said they had previously feared what their natural hair would look like. Tara (2012) stated, "I was at a different level than [when I was younger], and I agreed with what society said was beautiful." Being afraid of their hair texture was also a result of the fact that the participants did not know what it would look like, because they had not seen or felt it since childhood. In compliance with the White standard of beauty, straightening the hair became a rite of passage for most girls. Many African American women will never see their natural hair again, because they will wear a permed or relaxed hairstyle for the rest of their lives. In opposition to the White standard of beauty, Harriett (2003) stated, "You should not have to feel like you have to conform to be equal." As participants removed the sense of restriction the dominant society held over them, their lives began to change.

The data revealed multiple dimensions that enhanced quality of life and aschematic perceptions regarding the White standard of beauty. Figure 1 provides a representation of these dimensions. Going natural was liberating for all the women. Nia (2003) stated, "It was time for me to be *free!*" Elaine (2012) said, "I'm freaking *free!* I have more control over my hair now!" A prohibiting factor resulting from following the White standard of beauty

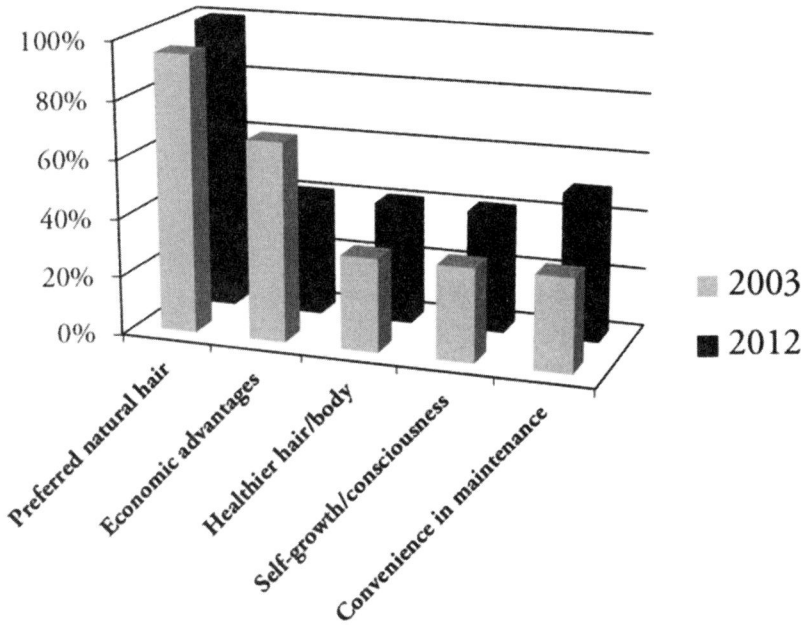

FIG. 1.
Quality of life
dimension
enhancement
for African
American
women wearing
natural hair.

emerged with discussions of the economic gains participants experienced when they wore their natural hair. Many talked about the beauty parlor visits every six to eight weeks, which could cost as much as $150 for a perm and cut. They also noted that they now needed fewer hair products, so they spent less money on maintenance and care.

Many explained that pressed hair, relaxed hair, and weaves restricted their livelihood. They said they could not go swimming, exercise, or try other physical activities because they were always afraid of ruining their permed hairstyles. Barbara (2012) stated that permed or relaxed hair is a "nemesis of most Black women." Perms/relaxers would burn the skin of some participants. One discussed second-degree burns and boils and explained how over-processing had made parts of her scalp dormant, that is a form of alopecia had affected the scalp.

Some described going natural as a spiritual journey. Kari (2003) stated, "I became a vegetarian about five years ago. I felt like it was time for a change." After cleaning her body by ridding it of unhealthy foods, this participant felt compelled to wear her hair in a healthier state and decided against perming it. Health was a primary motivator for many to wear natural hair. Brenda (2012) stated, "I want to be myself, and I want to be authentic, and health means way more to me than hair. And this [natural hair] allows me to swim, exercise, be *free!* . . . I grew tired of having my lifestyle fit my hair." Finally,

Abba (2003) exclaimed, "It's [natural hair] beautiful! Relaxed hair is just imitating another group of people." Through their "courageous" feats of going natural, all participants enhanced their quality of life.

CONCLUSIONS

The current study evaluated self-schema and self-esteem in connection with the life experiences of African American women wearing natural hair. Results revealed that these women tend to have high self-esteem regarding themselves and their hair. They discussed that they needed to have high self-esteem or be "brave" because of the criticisms surrounding wearing natural hair. Most, 67 percent, believed society does not accept natural hair. They also discussed how members of the African American community also tended not to accept natural hair because of their strong desire to fit into the White standard of beauty. For the participants, the importance of maintaining this standard was negated after they realized how much their permed hair limited them lives physically, personally, and monetarily. The participants with processed hair discussed being unable to keep physically fit and suffering burns from the chemicals. They indicated that their natural hair allowed them to be free to experience life's adventures without the fear of ruining their previously permed hair. Wearing natural hair "goes against the grain," and early in their lives, the participants were schematic regarding their hair and wanted to fit in with the White standard of beauty. They developed the needed esteem to ignore the mainstream standards. Various life experiences, such as becoming more educated about themselves and their culture, were positive influencers in self-esteem enhancement and/or maintenance. All participants agreed that their natural hair reflected their self-acceptance; however, many admitted having been afraid of wearing natural hair because of the internalized racism of the White standard of beauty's preference for "good" hair. Becoming aschematic of the mainstream standard allowed the women space to create their own meaning of beauty through a "counter-hegemonic strategy."

Most participants were in their forties, causing a single generational response to emerge in the data. Having a mixture of younger women and older women would have allowed for more diversity in responses. The data extending over a decade was also challenging because the author's data analysis style has changed. Future studies would generate valuable data by comparing the hair self-schema and self-esteem of African American women wearing permed/relaxed hair. In July 2019, the CROWN Act was passed in California. It would be valuable to have research data concerning how institutions and workplaces have changed due to the CROWN Act, along with the change in the microaggressions women face as a result of wearing their hair natural in this new era.

This research contributes to the field a richer understanding of the "freedom" many African American women have experienced with their choice to wear natural hair. It is hoped that, with this data, African American women wearing natural hair and those wearing perm/relaxed hair can develop a better understanding of each other to begin closing the cultural divide among them.

NOTES

1. Anthony Synnott, "Shame and Glory: A Sociology of Hair," *British Journal of Sociology* 30, no. 3 (1987): 381–413.
2. Cynthia L. Robinson, "Hair and Race: Why 'Good Hair' May Be Bad for Black Females," *Howard Journal of Communications* 22, no. 4 (2011): 358–76; Susan L. Bryant, "The Beauty Ideal: The Effects of European Standards of Beauty on Black Women," *Columbia Social Work Review* 4 (2013): 80–91; Cynthia L. Robinson-Moore, "Beauty Standards Reflect Eurocentric Paradigms—So What? Skin Color, Identity, and Black Female Beauty," *Journal of Race and Policy* 4, no. 1 (2008): 66–85.
3. Naomi Wolf, *The Beauty Myth* (New York: HarperCollins, 2002).
4. Robinson. "Hair and Race," 358–76; Cheryl Thompson, "Black Women and Identity: What's Hair Got to Do with It?," *Michigan Feminist Studies* 22, no.1 (2008), http://hdl.handle.net/2027/spo.ark5583.0022.105.
5. Tameka N. Ellington, "Social Networking Sites: A Support System for African American Women Wearing Natural Hair," *Journalism and Mass Communication* 4 no. 9 (2014): 552–64; Tameka N. Ellington, "Bloggers, Vloggers, and a Virtual Sorority: A Means of Support for African American Women Wearing Natural Hair," *International Journal of Fashion Design, Technology and Education* 8, no. 1 (2015): 21–29.
6. Ellington, "Social Networking Sites"; Kathy Y. Russell, Midge Wilson, and Ronald E. Hall, *The Color Complex: The Politics of Skin Color among African Americans* (San Diego: Harcourt Brace Jovanovich, 1992).
7. Ayana D. Byrd and Lori L. Tharps, *Hair Story: Untangling the Roots of Black Hair in America,* 2nd ed. (New York: St. Martin's, 2014).
8. Thompson, "Black Women and Identity," 843.
9. Jamie Ross, "BP Accused of Racism by Fired Top Executive," *Courthouse News Service,* Dec. 5, 2013, https://www.courthousenews.com/bp-accused-of-racism -by-fired-top-executive/.
10. Brina Hargo, "Hair Matters: African American Women and the Natural Hair Aesthetic" (MA thesis, Georgia State Univ., 2011).
11. Lanita Jacobs-Huey, "Gender, Authenticity, and Hair in African American Stand-Up Comedy," in *From the Kitchen to the Parlor,* ed. Lanita Jacobs-Huey (New York: Oxford Univ. Press, 2006), 71–88; Russell, Wilson, and Hall, *Color Complex.*
12. Thompson, "Black Women and Identity."
13. Hargo, "Hair Matters," 9.

14. Hargo, "Hair Matters," 6; Tracey Owens Patton, "Hey Girl, Am I More Than My Hair? African American Women and Their Struggles with Beauty, Body Image, and Hair," *National Women's Studies Association Journal* 18, no. 2 (2006): 24–51.

15. Cheryl Thompson, "Black Women, Beauty, and Hair as a Matter of Being," *Women's Studies* 38, no. 8 (2009): 831–56; Thompson, "Black Women and Identity?," 2008.

16. Saran Donahoo, "Why We Need a National CROWN Act" *Laws* 10, no. 2 (2021): 26.

17. Esther Akutekha, "How the Natural Hair Movement Has Failed Black Women: There's a Problem with Representation, Even among the Natural Hair Community," *Huffpost,* updated Sept. 16, 2021, https://www.huffpost.com/entry/natural-hair-movement-failed-black-women_1_5e5ff246c5b6985ec91a4c70.

18. A sample of twenty-five professional African American women with natural hair were interviewed in 2003 after Institutional Review Board approval from Michigan State University. An additional thirteen professional African American women with natural hair were interviewed in 2012 after Institutional Review Board approval from Kent State University.

19. Morris Rosenberg, *Society and the Adolescent Self-Image,* rev. ed. (Middletown, CT: Wesleyan Univ. Press, 1989).

20. Afiya A. Mbilishaka, "Strands of Intimacy: Black Women's Narratives of Hair and Intimate Relationships," *Journal of Black Sexuality and Relationships* 5 (Summer 2018): 43–61.

21. Eric Francisco, "How Tinder Accidentally Exposed Society's Inherent Racism," *Inverse.com,* Sept. 13, 2017, https://www.inverse.com/article/36379-tinder-black-women-asian-men-racism.

22. Damona Hoffman, "See How Black Women Are Dealing with Being Rejected by Black Men," *BET.com,* Feb. 12, 2018, https://www.bet.com/style/living/2018/02/12/here-s-what-it-s-really-like-to-be-a-black-women-looking-for-lov.html.

23. Thompson, "Black Women and Identity."

24. *Nappily Ever After,* directed by Haifaa Al-Mansour (Atlanta, GA: Netflix, Marc Platt Productions, and Badabing Pictures, 2018).

PART 3

The New Movement of Self-Acceptance of Black Hair

CHAPTER 6

Hair Apparent

AN EXAMINATION OF THE NATURAL HAIR MOVEMENTS OF THE 1960S AND THE PRESENT

Mikaila Brown

When I was growing up, my strict Jamaican mother never allowed me to perm (chemically straighten) my hair. Instead, the only styles she accepted were "age-appropriate" box braids and buns. As I grew older, I stayed the course because I felt my curly Afro complimented my activist tendencies. Because I was light-skinned with predominantly European features, wearing my hair natural was a signal to all around me that I was "down." For me, *down* meant being committed to the advancement of Black people and all related causes. I believed wearing my hair straight made me look too preppy, which was confirmed when I did get a blow out and friends called me Hilary Banks (the incredibly privileged and pampered character from the show *Fresh Prince of Bel Air*). I did not want to be associated with such a passive character. My understanding of my hair continues to evolve, but the one common thread is my belief that my naturally curly Afro acts as a billboard for my politicism. While my activism is more academic and less radical than the politicism of the Black Power movement, my naturally curly Afro has been, for me, a call back to that time.

In this chapter, I will compare the Black is Beautiful movement the 1960s to the current natural hair movement through an examination of the conditions that shaped these movements and the influence they had on hairstyles of the times. The expression of culture through hairstyles has been a long-standing signature of Black communities.[1] From Afros to braids, Black people have often used their hair as a personal expression of who they are and what they stand for politically.[2] This was definitely the case in the 1960s and 1970s, when the Black Power movement ushered in a period of explicit racial pride for Black people living in the United States. The Afro became one of the most identifiable markers of this new movement, signifying an explicit shift in how Black people saw themselves and their hair. It became synonymous with not only political change but also Black self-love, defining qualities of the period's social rebellion and civil unrest.[3]

The natural hair movement began in the United States in the early 2000s but has significantly intensified in the last ten years with an explosion in the number of social media communities and products catering to non-straightened hair textures. This movement actively encourages women of African descent to cultivate and maintain their natural Afro-textured hair.[4] It promotes self-acceptance of Black beauty (Afro-textured hair) and rejects the White standard of beauty (straight hair). Some have argued that the natural hair movement is more attributable to a rejection of unhealthy hair products by Black communities than a political assertion of racial pride.[5] However, the movement is a collaborative celebration of Black women supporting, encouraging, and educating each other about their natural hair. The main connection between the natural hair movement, The Black Power movement, and the Black Lives Matter movement (BLM) is the empowerment of the Black community.

This chapter also will explore the effect that racial tensions in the United States (since the summer of 2013—when Trayvon Martin, a young Black American was shot dead by a non-Black man) have had on cultivating a movement toward more natural hairstyles. It will examine the relationship between the emergence of social phenomena of the BLM movement, #blackgirlmagic, and powerful social media subgroups like Black Twitter and the new revolution of self-love through an acceptance of natural hair. This chapter will attempt to determine whether a correlation exists between the resurgence of Black radical movements, like the BLM movement, and the rise in the popularity within local Black communities to embrace a healthier lifestyle starting at their hair roots. Are contemporary Black women using their natural hair to signify their politicism?

THE POLITICS OF BLACK HAIR: 1960S AND 1970S

The emergence of the Black Power movement in the 1960s can be best attributed to the collective discontent of the Black underclass at that time. Many found the civil rights movement woefully insufficient to help Blacks living in dire poverty and dealing with racial violence. Leaders like Huey Newton of the Black Panther Party, Stokely Carmichael of the Black Power movement, and Malcolm X espoused Black nationalism, separatism, and the necessity of using violence as a means of self-defense against racism. They criticized Dr. Martin Luther King Jr.'s nonviolent strategies for not directly addressing the extreme racial violence Black people experienced at the hands of the police.[6]

The Black Power leaders drew their critique of cultural assimilation from thinkers like W. E. B. Du Bois and Frantz Fanon, who criticized the civil rights movement's attempts to integrate Black people into American society. Instead, they proposed Black nationalism, racial solidarity, and economic autonomy. They incited young Blacks to reject racist White ideologies and Eurocentric ideas, and this trickled down into the beauty standards of the time. The Black is Beautiful movement was the ultimate expression of a new racial consciousness. It was, as explained by bell hooks, a call to reconfigure "self-hatred into self-love."[7]

The Black Power movement mobilized the idea of Black bodies as a cultural resource to generate a new aesthetic to reconstruct Black cultural pride. If the Harlem Renaissance was inspired by the Black elites, the Black Power movement was designed for the working class. There were some overlaps, like a commitment to decolonizing minds and consciousness, but a critical difference was that this new movement reconsidered Black culture as a space of freedom and affirmation for working-class people, without their striving to be "respectable."[8] Black poets, writers, musicians, singers, and artists felt inspired to produce a new Black cultural aesthetic. They explored and rewrote African history and culture and challenged Eurocentric Western knowledge that characterized Africans as uncivilized, subhuman, and backward. Blackness was given a new meaning and a new symbolism to reconstruct Black culture, ethnicity, and identity in a more self-authored and positive way.[9]

The Black feminist movement grew out of the civil rights movement, stemming from groups such as the Student Nonviolent Coordinating Committee.[10] The Black Power movement, including the Black Panther Party, helped shape several radical Black feminist organizations founded between 1966 and 1970. Black women organized and led the strikes, boycotts, sit-ins, and marches, such as the March on Washington, and other important civil-rights campaigns. They also participated in and ran many community-based programs such as free health and breakfast programs for the Black Power movement. However, their experiences were often subsumed in the category of "Female" in the Black radical movements *and* the category of "Black" in the radical feminists' movement—not wholeheartedly welcomed in either space. Therefore, Black women developed a movement to represent the intersectionality of their identity and their societal concerns as Black women.

Black women's experiences of poverty, misogyny, sexism, and racism were glossed over and often not fully acknowledged in either the feminist or Black Power realm. The Black feminist movement not only grew out of these movements, but it was also formed in direct opposition and resistance to the pervasive sentiments of sexism and racism within each.[11] Black feminists felt marginalized by the Black Nationalists, who tended to embrace patriarchal values and often relegated women to traditional roles of mothering and caretaking. When the experiences of racism, work, family, patriarchy, and state violence of Black women differed from those of White feminists, these were largely ignored as not constituting a woman's struggles.[12]

Within the Black feminist movement, Black hair played a prominent role in communicating a radical message about the political identity of the participants. For some women, natural hair, specifically the Afro, was simply a fashion statement; but for many others, wearing an Afro signified racial pride and solidarity with Black radical movements. These movements also created cultural awareness of issues of gendered colorism in Black communities by challenging internalized racism.[13] For many years, naturally curly hair was considered shameful within American Black communities, and a major part of the coming-of-age rituals of little Black girls meant that they were taught the European ideal of beauty, which included straightening their hair. This indoctrination was so subversive that for many Black women, hair straightening was not explicitly seen as an attempt to look White but an essential part of their communal and social lives and an important step in a Black girl's coming of age. Many working-class women viewed getting their hair straightened in beauty parlors as entering a much-needed space of leisure and female bonding, rather than the assimilation tool that it was.[14]

The success of the Black is Beautiful movement is largely due to the Black Power movement creating space for an alternative understanding of these common rituals.[15] Young Black girls were surrounded by self-affirming caretakers, parents, teachers, and significant others who had a more awakened and self-authored understanding of Black pride. This validation of their natural, physical characteristics by significant people in their lives became a reasonable challenge to a generalized feeling of self-hatred. Also, the continued critique of systematic structural racism and discrimination, encouraged by the militant ideas of the 1960s, helped externalize anger and, therefore, protected self-esteem.

Black women's ambivalence to conforming to dominant beauty ideals and instead adopting an Afrocentric model of beauty was direct evidence of this shift. Black women were more comfortable dismissing images of attractive White women as unimportant and instead celebrating images of attractive Black women. A perfect example of this was the popularity of Harlem's own Grandassa Models, who were considered the pioneers of the Black is Beautiful movement.

In the 1960s, popular photographer and activist Kwame Brathwaite co-founded a group called the Grandassa Models. *Grandassa* was taken from the term *Grandassaland,* coined by Black nationalist Carlos A. Cooks to refer to Africa. Braithwaite was committed to creating images that made Black women feel proud of their hair and their Blackness. So, he hired models with skin tones ranging from light brown to dark brown, who had full lips, natural hairstyles, a variety of body shapes, and wore African-style clothing. This was a sharp break from the mainstream approach of promoting more Eurocentric models as the standard of beauty. Braithwaite's models' unapologetic celebration of their racial pride directly reflected the political atmosphere cultivated by the Black Power movement.[16]

THE POLITICS OF BLACK HAIR: TODAY

Five decades later, the same racial pride and in-your-face attitude of the Black Power movement is evident within the BLM movement. Sadly, the issues of fair voting rights, equitable employment opportunities, and an improved criminal justice system serve as the tenets of both movements, despite the significant passage of time. Law enforcement was a significant target of the Black Power movement, as evidenced by the carrying of legal weapons in public by the Black Panthers in the 1960s. Similarly, the BLM movement employs extravagant public displays to highlight the insecurity that Black communities in America feel around police. For example, during protests meant to highlight the injustices behind the murders of Breonna Taylor and George Floyd by police in the summer of 2020, protesters laid down in traffic on major highways in New York City and marched naked Black women down a San Francisco street chanting, "Say Her Name." The iconic image of the raised, black-gloved fists of John Carlos and Tommie Smith on the medal stand at the 1968 Summer Olympics in Mexico City directly parallels the videos of hundreds of BLM protesters, with their palms pushed above their heads, chanting, "Hands Up, Don't Shoot."[17]

Like the Black liberation movements that came before it, BLM has made racial injustice awareness and reinforcing racial pride a cornerstone of its mission. However, the BLM movement differs from the civil rights movement and aligns itself more with the Black Power movement by actively discouraging participants from playing down their Blackness to avoid mistreatment but rather encouraging them to lean unapologetically into it.[18]

As a result, BLM has affected the current natural hair movement similarly to how the Black Power movement influenced the Black is Beautiful movement. At its core, the natural hair movement is represented by a group of women providing encouragement, advice, product reviews, and hairstyle tutorials to other women interested in leaving behind the unhealthy chemicals used to perm Black women's hair. Started unofficially in 2005, with the debut of the critically acclaimed documentary *My Nappy Roots: A Journey through Black Hair-itage,* the movement found its roots (pun intended) in the over four hundred years of Black hair history, starting in Africa through the middle passage through the present-day evolution of the Black hair industry.[19]

An increasing awareness of the harmful effects of relaxers on the scalp has encouraged the return to more natural hairstyles by Black women. Women have suffered with intense reactions that result in itching, red patches, burns, broken hairs, and even alopecia.[20] Though the current shift to natural hair has deep roots in a healthier life perspective, it also has a political aspect. The BLM movement has spilled over into a newfound conscientiousness that Black hair matters too. The increasing popularity of social media and other online outlets have created an unprecedented space for stories about marginalized communities and their experiences, generating a newfound awareness of the stigmatization that Black people face because of their natural hair.[21]

THE POLITICS OF "PROFESSIONAL" BLACK HAIR

The politics of Black hair is evidenced by many media stories covering the discrimination Black women have faced in the workplace due to their hair. Alexis McGill Johnson, Rachel D. Godsil, Jessica MacFarlane, Linda R. Tropp, and Phillip Atiba Goff's 's article titled "The Good Hair Study: Explicit and Implicit Attitudes toward Black Women's Hair" speaks to the complexity of Black women navigating the social pressures of status and perceived class representation within their workplaces.[22] It is widely accepted that within professional settings, natural Black hair has been seen as low class, unkempt, and unacceptable, while straight hair is seen as professional, tidy, and preferred. A direct result of the discrimination and dehumanization Black people faced during slavery times is that they were taught to believe their African features (skin, hair textures, facial features) were bad. Out of that ideology and the mixing of races between White slave traders and their African slaves, "good" and "bad" hair emerged and began to create an intraracial divide among Black people. "Good hair is perceived as hair that is closest to White people's hair—long, straight, silky, bouncy, manageable, healthy, and shiny; while 'bad' hair is short, matted, kinky, nappy, coarse, brittle, and wooly."[23] Studies have shown that one in five Black women have felt social pressure to straighten their hair for work, which is twice as many as their White counterparts.[24]

A Black woman named Chastity Jones, who lived in Alabama, had a job offer withdrawn in 2012 solely because of her hair, worn in locs. The company ultimately won the lawsuit because a clause in its contract deemed Jones's natural hairstyle outside the realm of a "presentable image" and instead considered it an "excessive hairstyle."[25] Disappointing decisions like this reinforced harmful biases against Black women's natural hair, and they are not limited to corporate environments. In 2014, popular Black hairstyles like locs and cornrows were banned by the US Army's uniform regulations. In this ban, locs were described using racially biased language like "unkempt and matted," demonstrating the Army's lack of attempts to understand Black hair.[26]

In 2013, an Oklahoma charter school banned seven-year-old Tiana Parker from wearing her hair in locs. Her parents were told that her hair could "distract from the respectful and serious atmosphere [the school] strives for."[27] This incident, coupled with the proliferation of media stories about Black women working in the entertainment industry not receiving the same hair care options as their non-Black counterparts, exemplifies a growing awareness that Black hair is being unfairly policed by many established institutions and industries.

Title VII of the Civil Rights Act of 1964 allows employers to enforce appearance policies that ultimately regulate the hairstyles of their employees.[28] The Equal Employment Opportunity Commission states employers can enforce a dress code that calls for "neutral hairstyles," as long as it is applied to everyone equally, regardless of race.[29] This rule does not take into account that what is deemed "neutral" in terms of hairstyles is entirely subjective, nor does it consider a historically, pervasive bias against Black hair.

Black women experience many psychological and emotional losses when they feel forced to straighten their hair for employment purposes.[30] Changing to fit into a demanding industry often results in extreme anxiety for those striving to find employment to financially sustain themselves. It also functions as a psychological tool that encourages one to please others to achieve self-preservation.[31] By resisting the urge to conform to "expected" behaviors, even at the risk of financial instability, Black people wear their natural hair in professional settings in a revolutionary act similar to the call made by the Black Power movement in the 1960s and 1970s to actively reject a White ideal. Its revolutionary roots are made apparent by the fact that an increasing public defense of natural hairstyles like locs, Afros, and braids has resulted in the decriminalization of Black natural hair in both New York and California in 2019.[32] On July 3, 2019, California was the first state to prohibit discrimination against Black hair, and Los Angeles Democrat senator Holly Mitchell cleverly named the law "The CROWN Act" (Senate Bill No. 188). New York followed suit on July 12, 2019, when Governor Mario Cuomo signed into law "The Human Rights Law and Dignity for all Students Act (S62.094)."

Evidence of a wider societal impact can be seen in how Black hair has been covered within mainstream and social media. While natural hair discrimination has existed for decades, its coverage by mainstream media outlets has led to an uproar that directly feeds into the activist sentiment so prevalent today. The sentiment is only reinforced by the endorsement and adoption of the natural hair trend by celebrities, with popular Black actresses and musicians like Solange Knowles and Viola Davis proudly showcasing and discussing their love of their natural hairstyles. Colin Kaepernick, an acclaimed football player and prominent advocate for racial justice, wears his hair in an Afro, directly referencing the hairstyle's rise to prominence during the Black Power movement as a symbol of resistance. A preponderance of stories within mainstream media highlighting these repercussions shows that the BLM movement is using natural Black hair as a political tool in ways significantly different from those of the Black Power movement.

Members of the Black Power movement has always understood that they had zero input in how Blacks were portrayed within the mainstream press, so they never strived for general public approval. Instead, they created their own media outlets like the *Black Panther Black Community News.* Conversely, BLM is a movement developing in the age of personally curated content and social media. BLM has leveraged the popularity of its curated content, as well as a collaboration with the social phenomenon of Black Twitter, to further its agenda, establishing a significant presence in the mainstream media. This movement is much less worried about being misrepresented by the mainstream media than the Black Power movement was. BLM activists have a more prominent role in the narratives constructed about them, often using cellphone photographs, videos, and commentary to go viral on social media.[33] Some of the stories BLM has promoted to highlight the continued racial injustice within American society have focused on natural Black hair.

This heightened awareness around Black hair is complemented by a shift in images of Black hair within mainstream advertising campaigns. In the past, any representations of "attractive" Black women in media campaigns included only light-skinned Black women with straight hair. Vanessa King and Dieynaba Niahaly's study "The Politics of Black Women's Hair" explores the media's ability to influence national perceptions of different hair textures. The media's consistent portrayal of White women with straight hair as the standard of beauty meant that very few Black women felt beautiful if they were not conforming to Caucasian-like traits such as light or nearly White skin and straight hair.[34]

Samantha Yee Yee Fo's study "The Beauty Trap: How the Pressure to Conform to Society's and Media's Standards of Beauty Leave Women Experiencing

Body Dissatisfaction" confirms that women often unconsciously accept and internalize beauty standards that dominate "media-presented societal messages."[35] When society propagates messages that make young Black girls feel like their natural physical attributes are unattractive, they ultimately grow up to dislike themselves.[36] The harmful effects of negative self and racial perceptions have wider implications on the well-being of young girls as they grow up. A lack of representation within the media, the potential of rejection from jobs and partners, and possible negative repercussions from educational institutions can result in significant social, emotional, and economic harm not only to themselves but also to their families and communities.[37]

Even within publications that cater to a majority Black readership, like *Essence* and *Ebony*, depictions of fashion trends have historically included images of Black women with wigs, weaves, buns, and ponytails rather than their natural hair. Tiffany Thomas's piece "Hair They Are: The Ideologies of Black Hair" highlights that even Black-owned and-run publications whose media coverage focuses specifically on the political experience of Blacks in America have reinforced the marginalization of Black hair within their advertisements to reinforce a White ideal.[38]

This marginalization of Black hair is also evident in mainstream publications. This was made most obvious in 2007 when Ashley Baker, *Glamour* magazine editor, made a presentation to over forty lawyers in New York City titled the "Do's and Don't's of Corporate Fashion." Her first slide presented an image of a Black woman with an Afro, with the caption "Say No to the 'Fro!" She accompanied tis by commentary that included sentiments like "As for Dreadlocks: How Truly Dreadful!" She concluded her presentation by sharing her "shock" that common Black hairstyles were considered appropriate by some for the office. Rather, she described these hairstyles as "political" and in need of being completely given up.[39]

Since 2012, popular media and advertising images have shifted to include Black women, still predominantly light-skinned, but wearing their natural, curly hair. This shift, coupled with a proliferation of YouTube videos highlighting the maintenance and styling of natural hair, is increasingly reshaping the perception of natural hair.[40] A growing number of pioneering hair vloggers have expanded the awareness of the various textures within the Black community, not only for those within the community but also for those outside of it. These vlogs focus on educating Black women about their specific texture and the products that best serve them as well as styling tips that make natural hair much more polished and controlled than the Afro, which is much less curated. The rise in an entire cottage industry that explains these textures, coupled with an increased social media backlash against discrimination due to one's hair texture within the workplace, exemplify the changing political perceptions of what qualifies as "acceptable hair" within professional settings.[41] Not only has current Black activism set the tone for promoting Black hair in all settings, but it has also created a stage for protecting natural Black hairstyles, particularly Black Twitter's vigilant commitment to calling out the cultural appropriation of Black hairstyles.

The acceptance of Black hairstyles in the workplace and the versatility of these hairstyles have empowered Black women around the world to feel more comfortable and confident about wearing their natural hair. The heightened awareness around products that work with certain curl patterns has resulted in more glossy expressions of Black natural hair than ever before. New products now take Black hair from the traditional picked-out Afro to a shining, finger-curled version of the Afro. However, women wearing natural hair still face struggles conforming to a White ideal of beauty. Even when going natural, Black women still feel pressured to strive for the "perfect curl continually." In most cases, this curl pattern is perceived as a looser curl—typically found on a person of mixed-race heritage, rather than the coarse curl pattern associated with African heritage. Regardless, unlike in the 1960s, when natural hair was assumed to work best in the halo shape of the afro, today's media and beauty industries are more inclusive in celebrating and cultivating the diversity within textures of natural Black hair.

"DIVERSITY AND INCLUSION" WITHIN THE POLITICS OF BLACK HAIR

The shift toward diversity and inclusivity can be seen in perceptions not only of Black hair but of Black women, particularly the critical role Black women played in radical Black movements. Unlike cofounders Alicia Garza, Patrisse Cullors, and Opal Tometi, largely recognized as the leaders of the BLM movement, women of the Black Power movement like Assata Shakur (Black Liberation Army), Denise Oliver (Young Lords), Fran Beal (Third World Women's Alliance), and Elaine Brown (Black Panthers) did not receive credit. Black women, both their voices and issues, are heard and respected more today than in past movements.[42]

The inclusive nature of the BLM movement has had a significant and unique impact on the current natural hair movement. The Black Power movement was an unadulterated Black movement. As a direct rejection of the integration ideas that were the foundation of the civil rights movement, Whites were not invited to participate. That generation also found pride in countering cultural ideals that saw White as good and Black as bad. Unlike King's dream of Blacks and Whites living together in harmony, the mission of the Black Power movement was for Blacks to reclaim power from Whites to determine their own fates. This difference in mission between the movements is best evidenced by the fact that the Black Power movement's anthem was "Say It Loud, I'm Black and I'm Proud," and not "We Shall Overcome." It remains the most "in-your-face-to-Whites" movement in American history.[43]

The BLM movement is decidedly more inclusive. Its founders identify as queer women, something that would have never been accepted in the 1950s and 1960s. Non-Black allies have been accepted into the movement from the beginning, with Whites, Hispanics, and Asians laying down on the streets in protest right beside their Black counterparts. This inclusivity has acknowledged not only the diversity of those committed to the movement, but also the diversity within the Black community, in its members' opinions, responses, and appearance. Images of Black women on the frontline of the BLM movement, wearing their natural hair in various configurations of curls, contribute to a broader understanding of the political movement and all it entails, as well as the people participating in it.

Inclusivity has also contributed to a more international acceptance of natural hair than in the 1960s. Because of the Afro's links to members of the Black Power movements, several cultures outside of Black America saw it as a dangerous symbol of political unrest. It was banned in Tanzania in the 1970s as a symbol of neocolonialism and an American cultural invasion. Today, countries typically known for supporting a European ideal over an Afro-centric one, like the Dominican Republic, South Africa, and Brazil, are leading a new wave of support for natural hair products and practitioners.

THE EFFECTS OF CAPITALISM ON THE POLITICS OF BLACK HAIR

It is important to address how the monetization of the natural hair movement has affected the Black American experience, compared to the Black is Beautiful movement. Profit has played an evolving role in Black revolutionary movements throughout time. While the Black Power movement was mainly community founded and self-sustaining, the BLM movement received a mammoth $100 million grant from the Ford Foundation in 2016.[44] The Black hair business is equally as lucrative.

The first two self-made Black female millionaires, Annie Malone and Madame C. J. Walker, amassed their fortunes by selling hair-straightening products. George Johnson of Ultra Sheen and Afro Sheen fame would follow in Walker's footsteps in the 1950s by starting his own hair care line, Johnson Products, which would eventually be one of the first Black-owned companies listed on the US Stock Exchange. The Black hair care industry is currently valued at more than $2.5 billion, with natural hair products taking up the lion's share. It is estimated that by 2020, perms would be the smallest segment of the hair product market.[45]

The popularity of natural hair products began to rise in the 1990s and early 2000s when a small community of pioneering Black women began making the products they could not find in their local pharmacies. Based on their initial success, investments from major beauty corporations have made it possible for major retailers such as Target, Walmart, and CVS to carry natural hair products previously relegated to specialty stores, usually owned by Koreans. Today, Koreans monopolize most of the Black hair care industry, as most hair products are made in Korea, and the Koreans refuse to sell to Black beauty supply store owners.[46] The shift to Black-owned hair care lines has made it easier for customers to gain access to what was once considered a niche product, but it also forces independent Black-owned companies to either compete with corporations that have historically ignored the natural hair market for years or be bought out.[47] Equally concerning is the fear that the political empowerment associated with the current Natural Hair movement will become watered down. Previous radical movements like the Black Power movement were ultimately disabled through infiltration and cooption by outside sources, and the natural hair movement is at risk of following the same fate.

This has been the case for popular natural hair brands, like Carol's Daughter, which started in a kitchen in Brooklyn, New York, only to be bought out by L'Oréal in 2014.[48] Under new management, Carol's Daughter's products are universally considered less effective than they once were. The brand struggles to remain profitable after changing its focus to be more inclusive and less Black-centric.[49] As more mainstream cosmetic companies acquire small businesses operating within the natural hair space and push a more inclusive marketing strategy, the meaning, message, and impact of natural hair products has become compromised. These brands risk losing their base, leaving us with these questions: What can current movements like the BLM movement and the natural hair movement learn from the demise of their predecessors? And how can they avoid a similar fate?

The answer might be to follow the example of the first successful Black hair care brands. The benefits of Walker and Malone's entrepreneurial efforts were significantly felt by the Black communities they served. Walker was a philanthropist who generously donated to other Black businesses, churches, and individuals. Her company alone employed over a hundred thousand African American women. Malone encouraged women of the African Diaspora to see themselves as African first. Their accomplishments were inextricably tied to an acknowledgment of the significance of hair within the

African Diasporic community.[50] Currently, mainstream cosmetic companies are investing advertising dollars into the increasing number of natural hair influencers, public intellectuals, bloggers, and tweeters, which does affect the well-being of individual Black people. However, more work can be done to undertake initiatives allowing small natural hair brands to maintain their autonomy and hire within their community, resulting in direct benefits to individuals and the Black communities at large.

CONCLUSION

In the face of political oppression, Black natural hair is a common thread of unity within the Black diaspora and a beacon of belonging. The freedom to wear one's natural hair provides generations of Black people—accustomed to a consistent denial of their individuality and humanity—the opportunity to have a higher quality of life. The relationship between Black hair and the current political environment is embedded within a personal fight against laws, policies, and practices that uphold the criminalization of natural hair. Revolution becomes a rejection of any attempt to physically or mentally pathologize any individual whose natural DNA is denied.

In the past, the political roots for natural hair were much more apparent. On a personal level, natural hair was an opportunity for Black women and men to express pride in themselves and their race. It was also a communal understanding, with beauty salons being a critical part of Black women's hair journeys. Unlike the natural hair movement of the 1960s and 1970s, today women of African descent are increasingly choosing to wear their hair naturally with less obvious political motivations. For many, it is less about making a political statement and more about radical self-acceptance and the opportunity to embrace their hair in its natural, unaltered state. It is also more individualistic, with a more personal quest to understand one's hair texture and unique curl pattern, under the direction of YouTube vloggers from one's home. However, radical self-acceptance is a political statement, especially in the face of potential social, professional, and economic down-falls. Mainstream beauty standards are beginning to consider natural Black styles. It is up for debate, however, whether this change is because natural hair is trendy now or that mainstream society finally realizes that being inclusive is just the right thing to do.

The current natural hair movement can continue to be a huge factor in turning the tide against natural hair discrimination as long as a shift in the focus remains on self-pride and self-acceptance for the enrichment of the entire Black diaspora. Lori Tharps, professor of journalism at Temple

University and coauthor of *Hair Story: Untangling the Roots of Black Hair in America*, said it best: "It really was revolutionary to see twist-outs, dreadlocks, and braids without people necessarily trying to make a statement. . . . For Black women to have a movement around beauty is revolutionary."[51]

NOTES

1. Robin D. G. Kelley, "Nap Time: Historicizing the Afro," *Fashion Theory* 1, no. 4 (1997): 339–51.
2. Ayana D. Byrd and Lori L. Tharps, *Hair Story: Untangling the Roots of Black Hair in America* (New York: St. Martin's, 2001); Yolanda Michelle Chapman, "'I Am not My Hair! Or Am I?' Black Women's Transformative Experience in Their Self-Perceptions Abroad and at Home" (MA thesis, Georgia State Univ., 2007).
3. Noliwe M. Rooks, *Hair Raising: Beauty, Culture and African American Women* (New Brunswick, NJ: Rutgers Univ. Press, 1996).
4. Tabora Johnson and Teiahsha Bankhead, "Hair It Is: Examining the Experiences of Black Women with Natural Hair," *Open Journal of Social Sciences* 2, no. 1 (2014): 86–100.
5. Cheryl Thompson, "Black Women, Beauty, and Hair as a Matter of Being," *Women's Studies* 38, no. 8 (2009), 831–56.
6. "Message to the Grassroots," in *Malcolm X Speaks,* ed. George Breitman (New York: Betty Shabazz and Pathdfinder Press, 1965), 3–17; "Carmichael, Stokely," *The Martin Luther King, Jr. Encyclopedia,* Martin Luther King Jr., Research and Education Institute, Stanford Univ., accessed Sept. 27, 2020, https://kinginstitute.stanford.edu/encyclopedia/carmichael-stokely.
7. bell hooks, "Straightening Our Hair," in *Tenderheaded: A Comb-Bending Collection of Hair Stories,* ed. Juliette Harris and Pamela Johnson (New York: Pocket Books, 2001), 111–15.
8. Peniel E. Joseph, "Historians and the Black Power Movement," *OAH Magazine of History* 22 (July 2008): 8–15.
9. Shirley Tate, "Black Beauty: Shade, Hair, and Anti-Racist Aesthetics," *Ethnic and Racial Studies* 30, no. 2 (2007): 300–319.
10. Stanlie M. James, "Black Feminism(s)," in *Encyclopedia of Feminist Theories,* ed. Lorraine Code (New York: Routledge, 2003), 54–56.
11. Cheryl R. Hopson, "The U. S. Women's Liberation Movement and Black Feminist 'Sisterhood,'" in *Provocations: A Transnational Reader in the History of Feminist Thought,* ed. Susan Bordo, M Christina Alcalde, and Ellen Rosenman (Oakland. Univ. of California Press, 2015), 260–79.
12. Joseph, "Historians and the Black Power Movement."
13. Byrd and Tharps, *Hair Story.*
14. Chime Edwards, "The Impact of the 'Fro in the Civil Rights Movement," *Essence,* Feb. 10, 2015, http://www.essence.com/holidays/Black-history-month/impact-fro-civil-rights-movement/.
15. Ayesha K. Faines, "Did Natural Hair Kill the Black Hair Salon?," *Atlanta Black Star,* Sept. 1, 2015, https://atlantaBlackstar.com/2015/08/20/natural-hair-kill-Black-hair-salon/; Toni Morrison, "It Is like Growing Up Black One More Time," *New York Times,* Aug. 11, 1974.

16. *Kwame Brathwaite: Black Is Beautiful,* ed. Tanisha C. Ford (New York: Aperture, 2019).

17. Jeré Longman, "Kaepernick's Knee and Olympic Fists Are Linked by History," *New York Times,* Sept. 6, 2018.

18. Armond R. Towns, "Black 'Matter' Lives," *Women's Studies in Communication* 41, no. 4 (Feb. 2018): 349–58.

19. *My Nappy Roots: A Journey through Black Hair-itage,* directed by Regina Kimbell and Jay Bleumbke (Los Angeles, Virgin Moon Entertainment, 2006).

20. Judy H. Borovicka et al., "Scarring Alopecia: Clinical and Pathologic Study of 54 African-American Women," *International Journal of Dermatology* 48 (Aug. 2009): 840–45.

21. Marcia Mundt, Karen Ross, and Charla M. Burnett, "Scaling Social Movements through Social Media: The Case of Black Lives Matter," *Social Media + Society* (Oct. 2018), doi:10.1177/2056305118807911.

22. Saran Donahoo, *The Good-Hair Study Findings Report,* Jan. 2017, https://perception.org/wp-content/uploads/2017/01/TheGood-HairStudyFindingsReport.pdf.

23. Neal A. Lester, "Nappy Edges and Goldy Locks: African American Daughters and the Politics of Hair," *Lion and the Unicorn* 24, no. 2 (2000): 201–24.

24. Shai Alexander, "A Point View: Sometimes, I Am My Hair—Untangling the Nuances of Coiffure in the Workplace," *The Inclusion Solution,* Dec. 13, 2018, http://www.theinclusionsolution.me/point-view-sometimes-hair-untangling-nuances-coiffure-workplace-Black-women-natural-hair/.

25. Chanté Griffin, "How Natural Black Hair at Work Became a Civil Rights Issue," *JSTOR Daily,* July 3, 2019, https://daily.jstor.org/how-natural-Black-hair-at-work-became-a-civil-rights-issue/.

26. Brenda A. Randle, "I Am Not My Hair: African American Women and Their Struggles with Embracing Natural Hair!," *Race, Gender and Class* 22, nos. 1–2 (2015): 114–21.

27. Tracey Owens Patton, "Hey Girl, Am I More Than My Hair? African American Women and Their Struggles with Beauty, Body Image, and Hair," *NWSA Journal* 18, no. 2 (2006): 24–51.

28. Sex Discrimination: Employment Discrimination Prohibited by Title VII of the Civil Rights Act of 1964, as Amended, and the Equal Pay Act of 1963, Sex Discrimination: Employment Discrimination prohibited by Title VII of the Civil Rights Act of 1964, as amended, and the Equal Pay Act of 1963 §, https://www.eeoc.gov/youth/sex-discrimination#:~:text=Title%20VII%20of%20the%20Civil,sexual%20orientation%2C%20and%20gender%20identity.

29. "Section 15: Race & Color Discrimination," *EEOC Compliance Manual,* accessed Aug. 22, 2019, https://www.eeoc.gov/policy/docs/race-color.html.

30. Vanessa King and Dieynaba Niabaly, "The Politics of Black Womens' Hair," *Journal of Undergraduate Research at Minnesota State University, Mankato* 13, no. 4. (2013), https://cornerstone.lib.mnsu.edu/jur/vol13/iss1/4/.

31. Ernest M. Mayes, "Chapter 5: As Soft as Straight Gets: African American Women and Mainstream Beauty Standards in Haircare Advertising," *Counterpoints* 54 (1997): 85–108.

32. Ginia Bellafante, "The Decriminalization of Black Hair," *New York Times,* Feb. 21, 2019.

33. Latoya Lee, "Black Twitter: A Response to Bias in Mainstream Media," *Social Sciences* 6 (May 2017): 26.

34. King and Niabaly, "Politics of Black Womens' Hair."

35. Samantha Yee Yee Fo, "The Beauty Trap: How the Pressure to Conform to Society's and Media's Standards of Beauty Leave Women Experiencing Body Dissatisfaction" (MA thesis, Auckland Univ. of Technology, 2010).

36. Jeanene Robinson and Mia Biran, "Discovering Self: Relationships between African Identity and Academic Achievement," *Journal of Black Studies* 37 (2006): 46–68.

37. Johnson and Bankhead, "Hair It Is."

38. Tiffany Thomas, "Hair They Are: The Ideologies of Black Hair," *York Review* 9 (Spring 2013): 1–10, https://www.york.cuny.edu/english/writing-program/the -york-scholar-1/the-york-review-9.1

39. Johnson and Bankhead, "Hair It Is."

40. Latisha Neil and Afiya Mbilishaka, "'Hey Curlfriends!' Hair Care and Self-Care Messaging on YouTube by Black Women Natural Hair Vloggers," *Journal of Black Studies* 50, no. 2 (2018): 156–77.

41. Cameron Jackson, "YouTube Communities and the Promotion of Natural Hair Acceptance among Black Women," *Elon Journal of Undergraduate Research in Communications* 8 (2017): 45–53.

42. Eric E. Vickers, "Black Power vs. Black Lives Matter," *St. Louis American,* updated Oct. 5, 2017, http://www.stlamerican.com/news/columnists/guest_ columnists/Black-power-vs-Black-lives-matter/article_2be176f4–58fb-11e6-b379 -dbec0d5362b6.html.

43. Vickers, "Black Power vs. Black Lives Matter."

44. Deiana Abdel-Gadir, "Black Lives Matter Collects Almost $100 Million in Donations," *Famuan,* Mar. 13, 2021, http://www.thefamuanonline.com/2021/03/13/ black-lives-matter-collects-almost-100-million-in-donations/.

45. "Money Flowing into the Natural Hair Industry Is a Blessing and Curse for Those Who Built It Up," *Los Angeles Times,* Aug. 10, 2017.

46. Emma Sapong, "Roots of Tension: Race, Hair, Competition and Black Beauty Stores," *MPRnews,* Apr. 25, 2017, https://www.mprnews.org/story/2017/04/25/ black-beauty-shops-korean-suppliers-roots-of-tension-mn.

47. Chavie Lieber, "Is Carol's Daughter Selling Out or Growing Up?," *Racked,* Nov. 17, 2014, https://www.racked.com/2014/11/17/7568691/carols-daughter-loreal-lisa -price.

48. Janell Hazelwood, "L'Oreal Acquires Carol's Daughter," *Black Enterprise,* Oct. 22, 2018, https://www.blackenterprise.com/loreal-acquires-carols-daughter/.

49. Jackson, "YouTube Communities."

50. Rooks, *Hair Raising.*

51. Collier Meyerson, "The YouTubers Who Changed the Landscape for #Natural-Hair," *Wired,* June 18, 2019, https://www.wired.com/story/youtube-natural-hair/.

CHAPTER 7

Going Natural

BLACK WOMEN'S DIDACTIC HAIR CULTURE

Taura Taylor

From slavery to Jim Crow to current society, Black women find their social, economic, and occupational life chances affected by others' surveillance and scrutiny of their feminine attractiveness or lack thereof.[1] As such, Black women's observances and nonobservances of grooming and beauty norms are bounded choices structured by explicit institutional sanctioning and implicit social coercion. Currently, against a backdrop of beauty norms informed by the white racial frame, the worldview that centers on whiteness as superior and nonwhiteness as subordinate, Black women are deconstructing antiblackness and acquiring specialized knowledge and skills via natural hair.

The social and cultural capital attached to chemically altered, weaved, straight, and curly hair with a loose curl pattern (typical of someone who is biracial) is notable to Black women with and without natural hair. Thus, the increasing number of Black American women wearing their hair free of chemical straighteners is noteworthy, considering that the majority of the world's population has curly to wavy hair. Yet, straightened hair is a ubiquitous global beauty standard.[2] To wear one's curly hair unmodified by straightening methods stands in contrast to a socially desirable norm among Black *and* non-Black women. Via online communities, local support groups, national expos and international marches, popular press, radio and film, and a diversity of blogs and social media outlets, Black women have engineered campaigns to celebrate Black women's naturally curly hair. This chapter captures the impact of natural hair care information as a cultural artifact that reshape Black women's awareness of the systemic oppression embedded in hairstyle choices.

Although American beauty trends are not constant, with peculiarities of style changing seasonally, annually, or with each decade, beauty norms are consistently hegemonic and often obscure the falsity of choice and the politics of coercion. Feminist scholars have problematized attractiveness and exacting beauty standards as mechanisms of control, thus offering much data in theorizing structural constraints and social coercion implicit within beauty "options."[3] Furthermore, race scholars, particularly those using intersectionality, add that the choice-centric perspective minimizes social location, the role of embodiment, and the creative elements of institutional power to influence individual agency.[4]

For example, military and workplace grooming codes often include words such as *uniformity, pride,* and *professionalism,* conveying rhetoric of gender, race, and "socially generic" neutrality.[5] Professionalism typically conveys competency, certifiable abilities, and accreditations. However, embedded in the cultural scripts for "professionalism" are implicit assumptions of undifferentiated and unexceptional social status (also known as unmarkedness), which infer ness and androcentrism or, at the minimum, ness and heteronormativity.[6] Thus, grooming standards, which convey scripts for appropriate presentation of one's employable self and body, center the body, enforce racialized and gender stereotypes, and ultimately place undue burdens on Black women to adhere to grooming policies.

Scholars Ingrid Banks, Ayana Byrd, and Lori Tharps, Kobena Mercer, Noliwe Rooks, and Maxine Leeds Craig draw on historicity and critical race theories to pioneer research on the relevance of Black women's hair and the inequalities related to Black aesthetics.[7] In contrast, Lanita Jacobs-Huey pioneers an ethnographical discourse analysis of hair in the Black American community with a lens toward the language attached to hair and gender. Recent research by Saran Donahoo, Tiffany Thomas, and Alexis McGill Johnson and colleagues revisits the impact of colorism, pigmentocracy, and hair texture upon contemporary intra-racial idealized Black femininity.[8] Overall, these studies center on race and gender within the literature of body politics and examine the role of hair in the subordination of Black bodies.

Previous research has affirmed hair straightening as a means to meet beauty conventions and navigate negative consequences. More recently, a growing body of research has been focused on the natural hair movement. Popularly referred to as "going natural" or "being natural," the growing preference among Black women to renounce conventional straightened hairstyles and styling methods has been designated a movement by parties vested in the subculture of natural hair.[9] These parties include hair and beauty industry workers, journalists, vloggers and bloggers, popular press magazines, celebrities, and Black women and men who wear natural hairstyles and those who do not. From scholars researching the natural hair movement, we learn that natural hair has important implications regarding shifts in Black women's understandings of identity, social networks, community, health, self-care, and empowerment.[10] The study's point of entry is among these studies, adding that a critical dimension of the natural hair movement is Black women's resocialization and emergence as purveyors of a didactic natural hair culture.

THEORETICAL FRAMEWORK

The study considers that ensconced within Black women's hairstyle choices are allusive racial projects—concurrent conceptualizations and navigations of race.[11] It centers on the visibility of Black women with natural hair, employing systemic gendered racism and Black feminist thought theoretical frameworks to analyze Black women's resocialization and to substantiate the knowledge embedded in the process of going natural as anti-hegemonic to mainstream society.

In a society that normalizes identities, perspectives, and behaviors based on polarizing and hierarchical borders, stratification is often examined by main effects as opposed to interacting effects. For example, when considering racism, we understand that American society privileges the social, political, and economic interests of whites of all backgrounds above those of persons of color. However, American society has multiple systems of oppression and stratification. Thus, systemic gendered racism and Black feminist thought consider that within American society, there exists racist and sexist oppression, which overlap to create distinctly different outcomes for men and women of color.[12]

Systemic gendered racism and Black feminist thought are informed by many critical race, cognitive, and multicultural feminist theories. These theories explain inequality by underscoring the roles of race and gender as foundational to privilege and oppression permeating all US social institutions. Both theories draw attention to America's historical and foundational objectification of Black women's bodies. The Black woman's body has a legacy of being an object of commodification to be bought and sold. Black women's bodies are also objects of production in terms of labor, objects of reproduction in the form of breeding, objects of maligned gratification as the slave master's sexual victim, and objects of speculation as the constructed antithesis of whiteness and maleness.[13]

According to Adia Harvey Wingfield, resistance to institutionalized oppression in the form of counter-frames is also a gendered process. *Counter-frames* are resistance frames in that they are the conceptualizations people of color employ to comprehend and resist oppression. Through counter-frames, oppressed and marginalized people define social reality for themselves outside of the oppressive meanings perpetuated by the white racial frame—the wide-sweeping worldview of white superiority and Black inferiority.[14] white Americans still carry a fear of the counter-frames that people of color employ. An example of whites' fear of counter-frames can be seen in the discriminatory grooming and appearance policies of many corporations that deem culturally inspired hairstyles such as cornrows "too ethnic." Systemic gendered racism was used to engage in a critical analysis of first, how the white racial frame informs or constructs the ideal standard of beauty and how whiteness emerges as the ideal image of beauty in the United States; second, the institutionalization of the white beauty ideal and resulting marginalizing consequences for Black women; and third, Black women's conceptualizations of natural hair and Black aesthetics as a counter-frame. In addition, Collins's themes on Black women's empowerment, self-definition, and Black feminist epistemology further inform the analysis of natural hair culture as resistance to systemic gendered racism.

METHODS

Data Collection

The data for this study is a subset of a larger body of work taken from the researcher's doctoral dissertation. An intersectionality methodological approach was used to guide the initial collection and analysis of the self-reported perspectives of Black women regarding the natural hair movement and explore how participants come to produce pluralistic conceptualizations about the "epistemologies of everyday life." The research question that guided the exploratory study was this: How do Black women make sense of the popularization of natural hair in a society where straightened hair is dominant?

Sixteen deliberately chosen interview participants between the ages of eighteen and seventy-four and representing a variety of social locations across ethnicity, marital status, religious affiliations, age, socioeconomic status, sexual orientation, political orientation, and health or physical wellness were selected. The first phase of the study began with distributing a questionnaire online via SurveyMonkey. Along with providing descriptive information, the questionnaire served as an instrument for screening participants. In the second phase of the study, respondents were interviewed individually, with open-ended, semi-structured questions to probe participants and contextualize the preliminary responses gathered from the survey. Depending on each respondent's preference, individual interviews took place in person, via a video platform, or over the phone. Interviews lasted between thirty minutes and one hour and were audio-recorded. In the interest of confidentiality, all participants were assigned pseudonyms.

Data Analysis

The work engaged a modified version of grounded theory methods to analyze the data. NVivo software was used to complete the coding process. The modifications resulted in the use of visual diagrams, as well as video and written journaling to repeatedly interrogate and code the data for variables and theoretical saturation. An intersectional and cognitive sociological approach to grounded theory methods was used to perform the analysis. The researcher is an engaged, analytical instrument who uses their experiences and knowledge to interpret the constructed meanings that participants have applied to their world.

The researcher fuses their knowledge (experiential data) with details from the participant to conceptualize implicit meanings to evaluate or expand an existing theory or advance new theories. The researcher's knowledge as a natural hair care expert informed the analysis of participants' characteristics and hair-related experiences. In addition, the researcher relied on a synthesis of systemic gendered racism, cognitive sociology, and intersectionality to guide her interpretations. The six cognitive acts Eviatar Zerubavel has identified (perception, attending, classification, signifying, remembering, and reckoning time) were used, as well as cues related to the social location to inform the coding process.[15] During three phases—open, axial, and selective coding—various themes emerged from the data. As such, the principal theme created for this chapter while coding transcripts—didactic hair culture—was only one of many interpretive yet informative possibilities. The theme of *didactic hair culture* captures the instructive cultural process of deconstructing systemic gendered framings of Black women's natural hair, bodies, and choices.

FINDINGS

From their accounts of childhood grooming rituals, interpersonal interactions, and concerns for institutional norms, it became clear that the Black women in this study engage in a sociocognitive reasoning strategy to navigate intersecting racialized, gendered, and classed beauty ideals and grooming norms. They shared that the increased visibility of Black women with non-straightened hair has aided in mitigating social shame and discrimination against racially categorized Black hair textures and aesthetics. Moreover, participant accounts reveal a lost knowledge of natural hair care influenced by structural dynamics. Their accounts underscore an emergent natural hair epistemology and Black women as epistemic authorities.

Learning to Reject Black Natural Hair

Sojo, aged sixty-six, is one of two participants who reminisces fondly about her childhood hair grooming experiences. She shares that she "got through" the process and remembers grooming as a time of intergenerational "bridging," in which she and girl relatives sat in her mother's kitchen having their hair styled, observing how to part and braid, and all the while listening to older women's tales. Whereas Sojo's experiences capture the endearing racialized and gendered experiences that Rooks so warmly describes in her research, most of the participants' accounts of childhood grooming are marred with memories of disparaging, painful, and time-consuming sessions.[16]

Annelle is in her mid-thirties; she recalls feeling haunted by her family's disapproval of natural hair and how they might react to her decision to go natural while in her teens: "I had an aunt who was a hairstylist. I had bad dreams about what they would do to my hair if I let them help me transition. Very discouraging. The things that people say about quote-unquote nappy hair can be discouraging."

Similar to participants from studies conducted by Tameka Ellington, Latisha Neil and Afiya Mbilishaka, and Randle, the participants share grooming experiences that negatively influenced their self-esteem.[17] Annelle learned in childhood that kinky hair is perceived as unattractive and burdensome to groom. Shirley, also in her mid-thirties, wears her hair chemically relaxed and remembers lengthy and painful grooming sessions: "I think some of the restrictions are time. I know for me, I know I'm very tender-headed. So, I just remember like when, you know, my mom and my aunts used to comb my hair, and it just—I was literally crying. I'm like, I do not want wash hour. I want wash, like, ten minutes!"

She attributes the discomfort she experienced in her childhood and does now to being "tender-headed," a Black cultural label for an individual with an "abnormally" low tolerance for pain when getting their hair groomed. Tender-headedness is frowned upon, as it is perceived as a sign of fragility and an imposition on the hairdresser's time to accommodate. Notably, the stylist or the styling process is rarely considered the problem.

Across generations, Black women can collectively remember hair transformations that could last more than a full day. The routine usually included hair washing (shampooing), combing out kinks (detangling), and the eventual pressing and curling of hair while one was seated in a chair near the stove. This ritual was also often accompanied by burned ears, neck, and/or forehead. Some remember hair-braiding sessions involving heavy hands pulling and tugging on hair and scalp for the sake of neatness and hairstyle longevity.

The earliest experiences many had with their natural hair are attached to memories of verbal scolding about one's hair being "bad" or nappy. Sojo shares that she was the "press and curl" and "Bantu knot girl" growing up. By today's white beauty standards, her hair is "good"—not course or kinky. The researcher hypothesized that this was partly why she might remember her experiences favorably. Sojo's hair is like S-patterned cornsilk. Her strands are fine in diameter and texture and require lower temperatures to straighten. For women with spiral to tightly coiled hair, hair grooming was, and for some still is, emotionally and physically traumatic. To avoid the pain of grooming their dense, naturally curly hair and to avoid being labeled tender-headed, Annelle and Shirley, like many Black girls and women, learned to navigate the undesirability of Black hair via thermal (heat straightened) and chemical straightening.

To free mothers, daughters, and hairstylists from the time and agony of "bad" hair, relaxing (perming) became a popular solution. Furthermore, thermal hairstyles are particularly vulnerable to moisture. Once a young girl's hair is pressed, she is forbidden from getting it wet. This typically meant dodging rain, not swimming, and limiting activities that would cause her to "sweat in her head." Although Ruth, aged thirty-four years, had to wait until she was an adolescent to get her first relaxer, she was an anomaly among her peers, "I know, growing up, a lot of my friends, they got their hair first permed when they were like, seven-years-old, eight-years-old." Through chemical straightening, young girls and adult women achieved straightness that absolved at least *one* of their social "problems." Here Kamala, age forty, shares her transition from pressing to relaxer: "My mother started me on that when I was eleven. She pressed my hair on Sundays before school began for the week, and then at eleven, I had to go and stay with my aunt. So, she was just like, OK, let's throw the chemicals in your hair because it's easier to maintain. So that's where I was, and I was creamy crack all the way 'til [I decided to go natural] yes because I didn't know any better."

In his docu-comedy *Good Hair*, actor/comedian Chris Rock popularized the term *creamy crack*, his take on black women's druglike addiction to chemical relaxers despite their unhealthy consequences.[18] Chemical relaxers are categorized as either lye based (with the active ingredient sodium hydroxide) or no-lye based (active ingredient calcium hydroxide). The relaxers work by penetrating the protective cuticle layer of the hair to alter the protein bonds in the cortex of the hair. Although no-lye relaxers are gentler in chemical strength, both kinds may burn the scalp. Unfortunately, girls and women are usually encouraged to withstand the burning sensations as long as possible to "ensure" maximum straightness.

Having time to do one's hair can mean having less burdensome hair—that is, straight hair. Having enough time to attend to one's hair care can be distinguished across class, gender, and race. For example, hairstyles that require more time and products are perceived as feminine and/or upper class. As Robert N. Levine asserts in *The Geography of Time,* there is a strong message regarding the value of one's time and what one does with one's time, as well as one's social value based on how one spends one's time.[19] Despite professional achievements, participants perceive their professional security hinging on grooming standards that whites and men, are not subject to. Thus, as Black women move up the social ladder, they expend valuable financial and temporal resources to attend to their hair in grooming processes that take exponentially more time and resources than those of their white and male counterparts.

As an outcome of being labeled with "bad" (kinky) hair instead of "good" (straight) hair, many women develop lifelong behaviors that participants described as bad for their mental and physical health. Chemically relaxing one's hair and wearing weaves are two popular grooming styles now associated with permanent hair loss, among other compromises to Black women's health.[20] Unfortunately, the damaging effects of Black women's most popular grooming habits are normalized as unintended consequences to achieving beauty norms and social acceptance. In contrast, however, many Black women are reframing and becoming resocialized regarding natural hair.

Learning to Love Natural Hair

According to participant Nzingha, language—having a vocabulary—to describe hairstyles and the common natural hair experiences is what establishes a natural hair community. Historical trauma and having a natural hair vocabulary inform her perceptions of changes in the trajectory of natural hair and the formation of the natural hair community. Several participants in the present study attend to shifts in the Black community's receptivity to natural hair over time. In one breath, Nzingha characterizes and chronologizes the natural hair movement, reflecting on the stigma attached to going natural before the advent of a visible natural hair community, along with the lack of instruction on going natural:

> There's like, literally a community around having natural hair, and that's pretty awesome. That community didn't exist fifteen years ago. I mean, it might have, but the upsurgence of the Internet has really sort of exploded. When I went natural, I was fifteen, so almost twenty years ago I went natural, and

I got called a boy, like, what are you trying to do? My stepdad was like, "Are you OK?" like, concerned about my mental health because I chopped off my hair. But then it was like, well, can't afford to keep getting relaxers, so there was that, but I didn't have a community to tell me, OK, so, you're doing a big chop. I didn't have a big chop. There was no vocabulary around what I was doing to my hair. It was just, I was twisting it up, and it was just what it was. The current community makes it easier to be natural.

Nzingha considers structural constraints and Black women's agency in their styling choices. She indicates that slavery left many Black mothers and grandmothers, and thus Black women, disconnected from knowledge of styling Black natural hair. Specifically, she perceives going natural as a reclamation of lost and interrupted knowledge. As several participants illustrate, going natural includes learning how to style one's natural hair and what products to use. Going natural involves both physical and mental processes. In addition, Nzingha recounts the intergenerational trajectory of Black women's hair by turning a keen eye toward how historical oppression has altered the beauty norms and grooming skills of Black women:

Well, it makes me think of—it was either a video or an article that I saw that was talking about how Black women were—there were laws on the books in New Orleans, in Louisiana, making Black women cover their hair up, and then also shaming us for having—historical us—for having our hair as it was as well as shaming. We wear—historically us—would wear headwraps, and they were shaming that, and then when we wear our hair out, there was shame and stigma—or maybe not shame and stigma, but persecution, of the women who would wear their hair out. I have no idea where that was oriented at . . . some—I have no idea about that.

Nzingha uses her own biography and Black women's historical timeline to draw attention to hair as a site of personal struggle and Black women's cultural trauma. She refers to a "historical us" to demonstrate her solidarity collective Black womanhood. According to Jeffrey Alexander, Ron Eyerman, Bernhard Giesen, Neil J. Smelser, and Piotr Sztompka, "Cultural trauma occurs when members of a collectivity feel they have been subjected to a horrendous event that leaves indelible marks upon their group consciousness, marking their memories forever and changing their future identity in fundamental and irrevocable ways."[21] Nzingha not only unites her own experience with other Black women's experiences but recites a history of sociopolitical and legal struggles.

The law Nzingha is referring to is known as the "Tignon Law."[22] In the eighteenth century, the governor of Louisiana, Estaban Rodriguez Miró, passed a law that required Black women, free and Creole (French and African mixed-race people), to cover their hair. This was meant to control the bodies of women of color, and yet Black women found ways to make their headdresses into attractive and fashionable headpieces. Accounts of Black women navigating the ire of white women, the unwelcomed advances of white men, and their own desires for self-esteem and beauty aspirations are framed as trauma. Nzingha draws on the collective memories and historical accounts of Black women's institutional systemic oppression, exploitation, and degradation. Although she is unable to recall the exact source of the narrative of the Tignon Law, that she draws upon this information demonstrates a growing body of knowledge centered on gendered racialized structural constraints and, moreover, the increasing public access to a type of history often omitted by, or reserved for, historians.

Of particular focus for the natural hair community is the reconceptualization of the Black body as beautiful. From hair texture to skin complexion to body mass index, Black women affirm Black bodies and cultural aesthetics. Participant Kamala draws attention to the learning process of attending to one's natural hair but also the cognitive socialization in reimagining Black hair texture as beautiful:

> oh me, it's a . . . gosh, it's . . . I don't know; it's absolutely beautiful to me now. You know? It's freeing; it's . . . you're not bogged down by—I don't know, even though I've had to buy several products for natural hair,[laugher] and I've also made products, you know, like oils, and things like that, and putting tea tree oil, and just trying to figure out different ways to do my hair, it's just more so of a, it's just a freeing concept which I believe we should all adapted to a long time ago . . . chemicals may have not even come into existence had we been taught initially, from the beginning.

Kamala's induction to natural hair involves reframing natural hair as beautiful, freeing, and socially progressive for *all* Black people. Like Nzingha, Kamala attends to the historical oppression that prescribes the normalization of straightened hair and chemically relaxing among Black women. Furthermore, her laughter signals the inconsistency between having "free" hair and needing to buy and make numerous hair products to maintain natural hair. Learning to appreciate one's hair involves attending to details and histories that highlight structural inequalities Black people faced people but also deemphasizing encumbrances.

As Kamala begins her interview, it is clear that she perceives herself as an initiate to going natural, drawing attention to not only her own shifting perception of natural hair but also to the community: "But I'm starting to grow out of that hair hate is what you all are phrasing it." "You all" here implies an in-group Kamala does not see herself as a part of but feels judged by. Several other participants also share this perception of judgment, their concerns about the regularity with which Black women's bodies are visible for observance and critique and controlled by others, even Black people.

The Future of Black Hair

Having a beautician in the family may manifest various outcomes, such as cutting hair grooming costs. Most significant here, though, is the impact on Black women's constructions of good hair versus bad hair and their abilities to self-groom. However, having a hair "expert" family member in adds the imposition of others' direct and coercive authority over one's body. As such, young Black girls are distanced from the self-care of their hair and any new ideas they may learn from their peers or media about hair care. Kamala explains the source of her lack of familiarity with her texture:

> No. I had no—she would press it—"Don't touch your hair!" [laughs] That's basically how it was, so I had no clue. She would just say that she always had a really just a warm comb; it wouldn't be a really hot comb. She would always make mention of that, but of course, I could never touch my hair. The minute I would take a barrette out, it's like, "OK, woman." [laughs] I had no clue. So, when I did start the chemical-free journey in Colorado, I just had no clue what my hair was going to look like. I was like, it just looks nappy, and I was like, I don't like this. And so, went back. Then started up again and I was like, "No, this is me, this is not nappy, this is actually a great texture of hair, I dig it." Except for the shrinkage.

Kamala, who is of course not the only participant unfamiliar with styling and the texture of her hair, also shares that she has not put a relaxer in her daughter's hair. Although her mother pressed and relaxed Kamala's when she was younger than her daughter is now, she is cognizant that her mother did the best she could, but she can make different choices for her daughter. Her experience highlights how Black women today are mothering differently than their mothers did, and how central is social media and the natural hair community in the exchange of hair grooming information:

> Google is my best friend. Google and YouTube are my partners; they are my pals. . . . Anything anybody says, I'm just like, "Google." How to do this to your hair, how to do that to your hair. Even for my daughter, no chemicals have touched her hair. I told her, "When you get older, you can make the choice if you want to," but I'm teaching her love her hair now as it is, something that I didn't get—I actually try to pass on whatever my mother didn't do. I'm just

like, "OK, Mom, you did a good job, but I'm going to just tweak this a little bit," so the next generation can be a little bit different. She enjoys me putting the Bantu knots and things like that in her hair. "Well, Mom, why don't you put the twists in it?" She still lets me play in her hair.

Unlike in most participants' childhood experiences, Kamala encourages her daughter to embrace her natural hair and finds herself playing with her daughter's hair, an experience she was denied with her own hair. Playing in hair is how women like Ruth came to see their hair as accessories for their manipulation, versus objects for the scrutiny and control of others. Ruth has tried a myriad of natural hairstyles, wigs, colors, and a texturizer (a mild chemical relaxer). Her hair allows her to "play dress-up" and engage in creative expressions of femininity.

Although Kito, age twenty-five, does not yet have children, she too has strong ideas about her future children's grooming choices. She expressed surprise that I did not ask about grooming and children more directly:

One of the things that you actually didn't touch on that I was surprised you didn't touch on was natural hair as it relates to your interactions with kids. So, like, moms who are raising their kids and who decide what their kids' hair is essentially going to look like. I think for me, even though, ain't no kids anywhere near here, and it's not about to happen anytime soon, but thinking in the future, thinking about what my interactions with my kids are going to be like in the future, I know that I'm going to try to keep them natural for as long as possible. When I say natural, I mean I wouldn't even want to make the decision for them in regard to them locking their hair.

Participants not only reverse grooming choices made by their elders but also make different choices for their children and unborn children. Several participants even share that in going natural, they have influenced other family members to do the same, in an intergenerational reaching back of sorts. Dorothy shares a direction of intergenerational bridging different than what Sojo experienced:

Well, funny enough, my grandmother started going natural. Right. It's partially been because of me. She actually attributed her going natural to me, because she's seen how long my hair's actually gotten in its natural state, without me constantly—because I used to get a press and curl every four weeks, consistently. Every four weeks. That was part of how I got my hair to grow back after the damage from the perm. She attributed part of her reasoning behind her going natural to me, which was very interesting, because my grandmother's the exact same way. She got her hair permed, just like how my mom got her

hair permed. My mom's not going to stop anytime soon, I don't see that happening anytime soon.

Black women navigate tradition and social progression by filling the gaps
between material and nonmaterial culture. Participants discuss once feeling ostracized but now exchanging information or helping another woman
transition.

Several other participants remark on the current "trendiness" of natural
hair and how some women, particularly younger women, choose natural hair
for popular styles versus health and politics. For Michaëlle, age forty-five,
natural hair is a healthy convenience. Still, she recognizes its broader appeal to other women: "I think it's more of a convenience, and seeing other
people with it, that is making it OK. I think it's more of a fashion—a trend,
but I don't think it's going away like other trends." Billie acknowledges the
broad spectrum of reasons women are going natural: among them political,
monetary, popularity, and self-affirmation:

> I think to a lot of people, it is a social movement, because they're definitely
> trying to make a statement with their hair. But I think for some people, they're
> just seeing the popularity and sort of treating it as a fad, and that's not neces-
> sarily a bad thing, you know, you can do whatever you want with your hair,
> and like I said, it tends to be a little cheaper actually, depending on what you
> use and do to it. I'm not really sure, because I feel like some people are just
> like, it's a really big thing, and other people are seeing it more, and they want
> to emulate that. Whereas other people, it's a sign of self-love.

Billie considers the subjectivity and avoids assuming that all Black women's
reasons for going natural are the same. Further, she also avoids condemn-
ing Black women for the particular relationships and meanings they attach
to their hair.

Participants make clear that attitudes typically change before the behavior. Black women may spend months or years contemplating "the big
chop" before going natural. Seeing styles, doing research, and asking questions precede going natural. Survey results reveal that study respondents
are most likely to engage in natural hair care activities that orient toward
the care and styling of natural hair, such as purchasing, making, and using
products and exchanging hair care information online. Very few engage in
collective actions that require temporal resources, such as advocacy or activism around natural hair, attending natural hair workshops, and/or wearing
clothing or jewelry that celebrate Black hair The survey reveals a decrease
in many activities that captivated media attention from 2000 to 2015. Having friends and/or medical research affirm the benefits of going natural may

further provoke Black women to pursue the benefits of natural hair. Going natural involves various considerations, such as how to style one's hair and navigate the status beliefs attached to having natural hair.

CONCLUSION

The research begins with the premise that natural hair has not always been socially acceptable among Black Americans. In some spaces, natural hair is still frowned upon. As such, the contemporary shift in the popularity of natural hair yields the question *What is going on here?* What can the shift tell us about social change in the United States, and, more specifically, what can it tell us about cognitive pluralism among Black women? In this chapter, I explored the meanings Black women learned about hair prior to and leading up to the current natural hair movement; of central importance is their learned and internalized perspectives about the social meaning of hair.

Many participants' conception of the world is one in which their hair is a liability. This conceptualization is beyond idiosyncratic and reflects an intersubjective worldview about Black femininity. For Black women, professionalism, femininity, and politics of acceptance are tethered to historical white racist framings of Black subordination. Most of the participants in the study have postsecondary degrees, are employed full-time, have an average income of $50,000–$74,999, and reside in cities known for Black homeownership and career successes. From their accounts of childhood grooming rituals, interpersonal interactions, and concerns for institutional norms, it becomes clear that Black women engage in a sociocognitive reasoning strategy to navigate intersecting racialized, gendered, and classed beauty ideals and grooming norms.

It can be argued that Black women's lack of styling and maintenance knowledge correlates to the lack of social acceptance and institutional stigmatization of Black natural hair texture. Over 90 percent of cosmetology schools use the Milady curriculum, which only recently, in 2013, has produced a curriculum for natural hair care and braiding. Milady's curriculum remains an issue today. Black hair is often an afterthought. The company's standard curriculum teaches Black hair care only as an elective, not a required course.[23] The omission of Black natural hair texture from the required curriculum contributes to the institutionalization of straight hair as the styling "normal."

Furthermore, perception is defined by our senses. In Western culture, sight is given primacy in shaping perception. However, smell, hearing, taste, and touch also shape our experiences.[24] Experience of pain; negative comments or verbal scolding about their hair; and the scent of burned hair or the foul, rotten-egg smell of chemical relaxers shapes Black girls' perceptions about their hair and body. Such messaging affirms "bad" hair as hair that requires such agonizing manipulations to be presentable, unlike "wash-and-go" hair. Furthermore, these experiences demonstrate the duality of grooming as a luxury and burden as Black girls and women learn to prioritize presentability at the cost of self-esteem.

Participants explain that, contrary to assumptions, going natural or being natural does not mean one avoids grooming and styling. They construct being natural with a focus on unaltered hair texture, but hairstyling and coloring hair are considered normal and acceptable grooming procedures within the beauty and bodywork of being natural, which involve a phase of socialization in which Black women learn how to care for and style their hair. Having a community around natural hair involves the tutelage required to style and maintain one's hair. Most significantly, it involves a language and comprehension that affirms an emergent natural hair epistemology and the epistemic authority *of Black women*. This researcher argues that natural hair care information emerges as a cultural artifact of Black women's rejection of hegemonic social coercion.

Though an adequate amount of empirical data exists documenting the relationships between social inequality and appearance, the current natural hair movement is a new phenomenon in inequality and body politics. Similar to previous studies on Black hair and Black cultural aesthetics, the findings demonstrate that hair holds specific racialized, gendered, and classed meanings for Black women. The data revealed Black women's conceptualizations about status, convention, and others' coercive authority over their hair and body. As they recollect and elaborate on their hair grooming experiences, they shed light on their initial reservations about natural hair and their cognitive shifts toward going natural.

This chapter contributes to several sociological subfields, such as sociology of race, feminist sociology, and microsociology. Few studies have focused on the conceptualization processes employed by Black women in their daily navigation of hegemonic beauty norms and social conventions. Occurring with less frequency are studies that examine how gender and other intersecting dynamics inform beauty-related racialized experiences and worldviews that may inform everyday cognition and resistance. The study adds that wearing one's natural hair heightens one's perception of personal community and invites Black women to frame natural hair care information as a unique Black woman epistemology.

NOTES

1. Enobong Branch, *Opportunity Denied: Limiting Black Women to Devalued Work* (New Brunswick, NJ: Rutgers Univ. Press, 2011).

2. Sarah E. Medland et al., "Common Variants in the Trichohyalin Gene Are Associated with Straight Hair in Europeans," *American Journal of Human Genetics* 85, no. 5 (2009): 750–55.

3. Clare Chambers, *Sex, Culture, and Justice: The Limits of Choice* (Philadelphia: Penn State Univ. Press, 2008); Mary Nell Trautner and Samantha Kwan, "Gendered Appearance Norms: An Analysis of Employment Discrimination Lawsuits, 1970–2008," *Research in the Sociology of Work* 20 (2010): 127–50; Deborah L. Rhode, *The Beauty Bias: The Injustice of Appearance in Life and Law* (New York: Oxford Univ. Press, 2010).

4. Gail A. Dawson, Katherine A. Karl, and Joy V. Peluchette, "Hair Matters: Toward Understanding Natural Black Hair Bias in the Workplace," *Journal of Leadership and Organizational Studies* 26, no. 3 (2019) 389–401; D. Wendy Greene, "Black Women Can't Have Blonde Hair in the Workplace," *Journal of Gender, Race and Justice* 14, no. 2 (2010): 405; Nadia Brown, "'It's More than Hair . . . That's Why You Should Care': The Politics of Appearance for Black Women State Legislators," *Politics, Groups, and Identities* 2, no. 3 (2014): 295–312.

5. Richard Thompson Ford, "Bias in the Air: Rethinking Employment Discrimination Law," *Stanford Law Review* 66, no. 6 (2014): 1381–421.

6. Wayne Brekhus, "A Sociology of the Unmarked: Redirecting Our Focus," *Sociological Theory* 16, no. 1 (1998): 34–51.

7. Ingrid Banks, *Hair Matters: Beauty, Power, and Black Women's Consciousness* (New York: New York Univ. Press, 2000); Ayana D. Byrd and Lori L. Tharps, *Hair Story: Untangling the Roots of Black Hair in America,* 2nd. ed. (New York: St. Martin's, 2014); Kobena Mercer, "Black Hair/Style Politics," in *Black British Culture and Society: A Text Reader,* ed. Kwesi Owusu (London: Routledge, 2000), 111–21; Noliwe M. Rooks, *Hair Raising: Beauty, Culture, and African American Women* (New Brunswick, NJ: Rutgers Univ. Press, 1996); Maxine Leeds Craig, *Ain't I a Beauty Queen? Black Women, Beauty, and the Politics of Race* (New York: Oxford Univ. Press, 2002).

8. Saran Donahoo, "Owning Black Hair: The Pursuit of Identity and Authenticity in Higher Education," in *Navigating Micro-Aggressions Toward Women in Higher Education,* ed. Ursula Thomas (Hershey, PA: IGI Global, 2019), 73–95; Tiffany Thomas, "'Hair' They Are: The Ideologies of Black Hair," *York Review* 9 (2013): 1–10; Alexis McGill Johnson et al., "The 'Good Hair' Study: Explicit and Implicit Attitudes toward Black Women's Hair," *Perception Institute,* 2017, https://perception.org/publications/goodhairstudy/; Lanita Jacobs-Huey, *From the Kitchen to the Parlor: Language and Becoming in African American Women's Hair Care* (New York: Oxford Univ. Press, 2006).

9. Mintel Press Team, "Natural Hair Movement Drives Sales of Styling Products in US Black Haircare Market," *Mintel,* 2015, https://www.mintel.com/press-centre/beauty-and-personal-care/natural-hair-movement-drives-sales-of-styling-products-in-us-black-haircare-market; Joyce M. Nimocks, "The Natural Hair Movement as a Platform for Environmental Education" (BA thesis, Pomona College, 2015).

10. Tameka N. Ellington, "Social Networking Sites: A Support System for African-American Women Wearing Natural Hair," *International Journal of Fashion Design, Technology and Education* 8, no. 1 (2015): 21–29; H. Shellae Versey, "Centering Perspectives on Black Women, Hair Politics, and Physical Activity," *American Journal of Public Health* 104, no. 5 (2014): 810–15; Raechele Cochran Gathers et al., "Hair Grooming Practices and Central Centrifugal Cicatricial Alopecia," *Journal of the American Academy of Dermatology* 60, no. 4 (2009): 574–78; Latisha Neil and Afiya Mbilishaka, "'Hey Curlfriends!' Hair Care and Self-Care Messaging on YouTube by Black Women Natural Hair Vloggers," *Journal of Black Studies* 50, no. 2 (2019): 156–77; Teiahsha Bankhead and Tabora A. Johnson, "Self Esteem, Hair Esteem and Black Women with Natural Hair," *International Journal of Education and Social Science* 1 (2014): 92–102; Brenda A. Randle, "I Am Not My Hair: African American Women and Their Struggles with Embracing Natural Hair!," *Race, Gender & Class* 22, nos. 1–2 (2015): 114–21.

11. Michael Omi and Howard Winant, *Racial Formation in the United States* (London: Routledge, 2014).

12. Adia Harvey Wingfield, *Doing Business with Beauty: Black Women, Hair Salons, and the Racial Enclave Economy* (Washington, DC: Rowman & Littlefield, 2008); Patricia Hill Collins, *Black Feminist Thought: Knowledge, Consciousness, and the Politics of Empowerment* (New York: Routledge, 2000); Kimberlé Crenshaw, "Mapping the Margins: Intersectionality, Identity Politics, and Violence against Women of Color," *Stanford Law Review* 43, no. 6 (1991): 1241–99.

13. Michael Bennett and Vanessa D. Dickerson, *Recovering the Black Female Body: Self-Representations by African American Women* (New Brunswick, NJ: Rutgers Univ. Press, 2001); Patricia Hill Collins, *Black Sexual Politics: African Americans, Gender, and the New Racism* (New York: Routledge, 2004).

14. Joe R. Feagin, *The White Racial Frame Centuries of Racial Framing and Counter-Framing: Centuries of Racial Framing and Counter-Framing* (New York: Routledge, 2010).

15. Eviatar Zerubavel, *Social Mindscapes: An Invitation to Cognitive Sociology* (Cambridge, MA: Harvard Univ. Press, 1997).

16. Rooks, *Hair Raising*.

17. Ellington, "Social Networking Sites"; Neil and Mbilishaka, "Hey Curlfriends!," Randle, "I Am not My Hair."

18. *Good Hair,* directed by Jeff Stilson (New York: HBO Films, 2009), DVD.

19. Robert N. Levine, *A Geography of Time: On Tempo, Culture, and the Pace of Life* (New York: Basic Books, 2008).

20. Jerry Shapiro, "Hair Loss in Women," *New England Journal of Medicine* 357, no. 16 (Oct. 18, 2007): 1620–30; Aline Tanus et al., "Black Women's Hair: The Main Scalp Dermatoses and Aesthetic Practices in Women of African Ethnicity," *Anais Brasileiros de Dermatologia* 90, no. 4 (2015): 450–65; Gathers et al., "Hair Grooming Practices."

21. Jeffrey C. Alexander et al., *Cultural Trauma and Collective Identity* (Oakland: Univ. of California Press, 2004).

22. Lisa Ze Winters, *The Mulatta Concubine: Terror, Intimacy, Freedom, and Desire in the Black Transatlantic* (Athens: Univ. of Georgia Press, 2016).

23. Arlene Alpert, Margrit Altenburg, and Diane Bailey, *Milady's Standard Cosmetology* (Boston: Cengage Learning, 2002).

24. Richard Nisbett, *The Geography of Thought: How Asians and Westerners Think*

Differently (New York: Simon & Schuster, 2010); Oyèrónkẹ́ Oyěwùmí, *The Invention of Women: Making an African Sense of Western Gender Discourses* (Minneapolis: Univ. of Minnesota Press, 1997).

TAURA TAYLOR

CHAPTER 8

The Evolution of the Natural Hair Movement in Virtual Space

AN ANALYSIS OF DIGITAL PLATFORMS, AGENCY, AND IMPACT

Lauren Cross

Online communities that support Black women wearing natural hairstyles have been in existence since the early 2000s, when blogs, other websites, and social networking sites emerged as democratizing platforms within American visual and media culture. The internet, as a space for online activism and counterculture knowledge, has encouraged a generation of Black women to publicly contribute visual pedagogies that reclaimed the oral traditions of African-inspired hair care traditions. Black women who use social media platforms like blogs, YouTube, and Instagram to challenge, influence, and inspire the appreciation of Afrocentric hair have been named Afro-cyberellas. The term was coined as an expansion on Nancy Hafkin and Sophia Huyer's theory of the cyberella, used to describe the impact of a woman's presence in a knowledge society.[1] According to Hafkin and Huyer, a "cyberella is fluent in the uses of technology, comfortable using and designing computer technology and communication equipment and software, and in working in virtual spaces." Hafkin and Huyer argue that cyberellas use innovation while distributing collected knowledge into the multimedia cyber world. Cyberellas use technology to challenge social pressures by improving the lives of other women. In a society where Black women's presence within technology and STEM fields is so limited, underrepresented, and underrecognized, Afro-cyberellas are Black women who acquire and use their knowledge of design, photography, videography, and social media to give other Black women the inspiration and the freedom to explore their tightly curled hair textures.[2]

In this chapter, the author analyzes the historical and visual discourse embedded in select digital platforms, from blogs to social media platforms like YouTube and Instagram, that have chronicled the natural hair movement from the early 2000s to the present. Additionally, this research evaluates the user-oriented approaches featured within each platform, measuring how different platforms have created a variety of visual influences.

BLACK HAIR DIGITAL BOOM

The increase in popularity of Black women wearing natural hair due to the social media boom indicates that digital media representation matters, where natural hair styling has moved from the margins to the center. The transformation of beauty standards among Black women suggests that a natural hair movement in virtual space affects real-world situations beyond the web. Black women creating natural hair knowledge online initially used their skills to develop independently owned and designed sites with their own brand identity. Over the past few decades, Black women have had an increased presence on social networking sites like YouTube and Instagram, posting videos and photographs of themselves and other Black women with natural hair. YouTube and Instagram are both social media sites where everyday people with access to the internet can post quasi-professional image content that is accessible to anyone interested in viewing. While the content on YouTube and Instagram can range from videos that might be featured on *America's Funniest Home Videos* to smartphone images of Sunday brunch, these mainstream social media sites are spaces where Black women have raised the awareness of natural hair care by sharing their knowledge, strategies, and life experiences while exploring African-inspired hair styling techniques.

In this way, social media platforms have become what Latoya Lee calls "virtual homeplaces," which are "affirming, counter-disciplinary, and trans-formational" as they allow Black women the space to "reenvision their body within restricting and dominating forces."[3] Likewise, scholars have argued that social networking sites provide a support system for Black women wearing their hair natural.[4] As a result, the imagery shared in these virtual spaces has become a rich area for visual analysis. Social media platforms display thoughtfully curated displays of images that become "a collage, mainly of headshots, self-portraits, and selfies" that are connected to hashtagged terms such as *#naturalhair*.[5] Social media profile names and hashtags become affirmations that empower Black women to boldly wear their hair in its natural, textured state.[6]

The natural hair movement online is influential because the public nature of social media platforms can create a sense of celebrity status.[7] The high volume of views, subscribers, and followers that propel the natural hair community what makes participation in it most compelling.[8] The representation of natural hair across digital media has evolved over the past decade. At the beginning of the natural hair movement, independently run blogging websites were the centralized spaces where Black women could find content representing natural hairstyles. Original sites like Nappturality.com were among the first online spaces created to share natural hairstyling ideas and provide discussion forums for Black women to share their experiences with "going natural." Later, other platforms like YouTube and Instagram, which were increasingly used as still and moving images became more compelling tools for Black women to learn about new hairstyles and products and to enhance their self-esteem about hair texture.

Writer Jamila Bey was one of the first to credit the influence of social media platforms as sites that made other Black women aware of the "practicality" of natural hair care.[9] Before social media, Black women had few spaces for learning about natural hair styling outside Black hair salons, which still prioritize such notions of beauty such as long, bone-straight hair. Also, Black beauty shops practicing natural hair styling methods are considered so much more expensive than traditional hair establishments that DIY tutorials in online spaces have quickly become a more feasible and economical solution. Now that social media platforms have are so popular as a "low-cost enterprise for black consumers," the places Black women navigate within the virtual natural hair movement have evolved from independently owned websites and blogs to mainstream platforms like YouTube and Instagram.[10] This is not to say that Black women no longer visit Black-run sites but, rather, that the virtual stage that Black women visit to deepen their understanding and acceptance of natural hair has expanded.

BLACK HAIR POLITICS

Black women contributing to the natural hair movement are exercising Black feminist and womanist frameworks through social and new media, bridging the gap between the rhetoric of natural hair, transforming hair politics, and creating a deeper understanding of natural hair care. One popular hashtag that has emerged across social media platforms from Twitter to Instagram to describe the evolution of the natural hair movement is #TeamNatural, which scholar Tiffany Gill has explored through the landscape of Black beauty and activism among Black women through social media and beauty shop culture.[11] In "#TeamNatural: Black Hair and the Politics of Community in Digital Media," Gill discusses the impact digital media has made on Black beauty politics, particularly in the imagery that is interconnected online through hashtags. According to Gill, hashtags like this are "ubiquitous on social media sites like Pinterest, Tumblr, and Instagram and can be considered both a declaration of pride and a source of contention among Black women, especially against those who represent for the oppositionally situated #Team-Relaxed, the term Team Natural has moved beyond the digital space, into the marketplace and beyond, complete with T-shirts and bumper stickers."[12]

While *#TeamNatural* does not define all Black women participating in the natural hair movement, the term most accurately describes the collective efforts of a community of Black women seeking to challenge negative perspectives of natural hair. These social media contributors have created what Gill describes as "a massive interactive archive of images of women with natural hairstyles," which are cataloged under various hashtags and "provide unique insight into the complexities of community-building around a supposedly common aesthetic."[13] These representations of Black women wearing natural hair communicate an acceptance of natural hair within virtual spaces that do not typically exist within traditional offline frameworks. These digital platforms allow for the reestablishment of new ideals toward Black hair that extend beyond the historical use of chemical relaxers and hair straightening.[14] Not only are natural hair blogs and social media sites are not only tools for social support for Black women, but they also communicate positive visual narratives about natural hair.

Regarding Black hair research, most scholars "debunk the idea that Black hair is no longer political" or "just hair." In "Black Women, Beauty, and Hair as a Matter of Being," scholar Cheryl Thompson makes the case that Black hair is not an unpolitical medium of expression: "It is not enough for Black women to simply wear their hair any way they please without their styling choice being called into question"; specifically, Black hair will only be "just hair" when systematic, political, and institutionalized effects of wearing Black hair are eliminated.[15] Other scholars agree and have discussed in their work how African American women and girls have been penalized for, as Noliwe Rooks mentions, wearing their race wrong.[16]

RESEARCH QUESTIONS

The overarching research question was to understand *how the natural hair movement in virtual space has changed over time?* Social media practice and activism are constantly shifting with an ever-changing culture of new technology trends impacting the features and web resources available in digital spaces.[17] For example, within our rapidly changing digital world, sites and contributors are present one day and gone the next, making it exceptionally necessary to document the evolving content on the internet.

The constant modifications in online culture also require us to ask additional questions: What elements or features make certain digital platforms, like YouTube, so consistent in their user-friendly design, experience, and practice for Black women seeking inspirational spaces online? What new marketing and promotional needs do sites like Instagram provide Black women advocating for natural hair and pursuing entrepreneurial possibilities within the natural hair community? Finally, while online spaces featuring natural hair began as areas of empowerment of Black women, it is vital to question why certain features like comment sections and forums evoke policing practices and hostility toward other Black women? These questions help researchers unpack how the digital platforms of the natural hair movement have altered as forms of agency and have changed over time.

THEORETICAL FRAMEWORKS

Black feminist and womanist thought are key theoretical frameworks applied to the analysis of visual images and content on Black women's social media sites. These social change perspectives are appropriate, because they are both theories created by Black women for Black women to describe the specific experiences and approaches they use to transform the world. Black women have used Black feminism and its extended branches, Afrocentric and African feminism to address the politics of Black hair because of their epistemological function to recenter African-inspired knowledge.[18]

Black feminism acknowledges that Black hair contributes to an ongoing political dialogue. Black feminist scholars suggest that when Black women choose to wear natural hairstyles, they are declaring affirmation of a personal style and value of Black hair. In "Releasing the Pursuit of Bouncin' and Behavin' Hair," Shauntae Brown White describes Black women's decision to wear natural hair as a conscious choice to redefine cultural identity, attitude, and interconnections among cultural politics, beauty, and hair. White uses "Afrocentric feminist thought," or Black feminism, as a framework that supports Black women in their decision to wear their hair natural while centering on their individual experiences and voices and as a tool to disconnect from cultural norms of beauty perpetuated by mainstream culture.[19]

Likewise, a womanist standpoint champions a similar agency of resistance and activism exhibited by "everyday" Black women. Alice Walker, who popularized the term *womanism,* described wearing natural hair as representative of personal transformation and well-being. Once she allowed her hair "to grow, [and] to be itself," she became free to grow mentally and spiritually without the oppressive restrictions of society.[20] Black women wearing their hair naturally within social media networks are, thus, displaying daily activism when publishing Afrocentric hair care tips and self-advocacy online.[21] Womanism celebrates culture and heritage and connects social justice implications with other creative expressions.[22] Social media is an avenue for womanism's do-it-yourself methods, which require neither the validation nor the participation of institutional powers.[23]

In her essay "In Search of My Mother's Gardens," Alice Walker reflects on the restricted yet powerful places where Black women can express their creativity every day.[24] Black feminist and womanist thought gives needed agency and autonomy for Black women to take control over the messages about Black hair via social media, which have moved into television, movies, and other media. While earlier generations of Black women had limited creative opportunities to challenge the status quo, social media has expanded the realm of influence for Black women's creativity within the cyber world. Black women are now curating the ideology of what it means to be a beautiful Black woman who is empowered to wear natural hairstyling that is not always accepted by society. Black women are using their access to the internet—through a computer, a smartphone, a blog, and or a social media account—to increase the visibility of natural hair care knowledge to other Black women.

METHODS

The natural hair movement in virtual space is a vast community of Black women exchanging hair care knowledge. Each social media site offers a variety of assets that benefit the natural hair community and elevate the perception of natural hair within society. To better understand how the movement has evolved in its content and platforms over time, this researcher conducted a visual content and image analysis.

Sites and platforms were selected for their popularity and their high volume of visitors. Websites Nappturality.com and CurlyNikki.com represent the beginning of the natural hair movement because of the vast numbers of visitors they received at the infancy of the natural hair trend of the early to mid-2000s. YouTubers like Naptura185 were selected to illustrate the midpoint of the movement, between 2008 and 2010. When the natural hair movement began, both YouTube and YouTube vloggers slowly rose in popularity. The steady growth of YouTube as a social media platform in general, and the specific rise in the profile of Naptura185 from a few hundred followers to 1 million shows the power of moving images as a form of digital storytelling that moved natural hairstyling trends from the margins to the center.

Within the evolution of social media practices, the Instagram platform represents the current state of the natural hair movement: it has evolved from blog posts and long styling videos to short, photographic affirmations. The shift to Instagram reflects the platform's popularity within American society over other social media sites and the online natural hair community entrepreneurs' need for marketable imagery Instagram profiles were selected for the analysis because of their connection to the #naturalhair hashtag and their large quantities of followers.

Each site and platform in the study was analyzed using rhetorical and user experience analysis. While rhetorical analysis explores how the images communicate, user experience analysis considers the journey the user encounters on the platform. Examining how Black women come in contact with images and platforms championing natural hair online can provide insight into how the visual narratives and experiences of the natural hair movement online have shifted.

VISUAL ANALYSIS OF DIGITAL PLATFORMS

Visual content analysis derives meaningful descriptors for image and video data. The following visual content analysis examines the evolution of online platforms that support the natural hair movement in virtual space. The analysis will begin by reviewing the visual representation and content of natural hair on Nappturality.com and CurlyNikki.com. It will then examine the content of Black women on YouTube and Instagram while uncovering data about hashtags and their overall influence on the natural hair movement. Figure 1 represents the initial popularity of various Black hair platforms.

RESULTS

When analyzing the visual representation of natural hair content online, four themes emerged that inform these platforms: first, they provide a safe virtual space for Black women to receive virtual affirmation and encouragement regarding their choice to wear their hair naturally; second, they host virtual forums to discuss Black hair. both for informative purposes and to address challenges within the community; third, they create virtual access to hair care knowledge, and fourth, they provide opportunities to engage in digital storytelling.

Online natural hair content provides virtual safe spaces for the discussion and appreciation of Black hair. Natural content on websites, YouTube, and Instagram creates unique platforms that make space for the specific experiences of Black women. While these virtual safe spaces have evolved from individual websites like Nappturality.com and CurlyNikki.com to major social networking sites like Facebook, Twitter, YouTube, and Instagram, online virtual spaces are crucial in the ways they allow Black women to build social networks around natural hair care. In their senses of cultural exclusivity, these spaces range from sites that identify as "independently Black," like Nappturality.com, to sites that have a transcultural audience, allowing for virtual advocacy to extend beyond intimate, safe spaces to more public ones.

CurlyNikki.com is a popular blog run by psychologist Nikki Walton, who explores natural hair styling tips and the emotional experiences of wearing natural hair. Walton created the site in 2008; since then, it has "more than 3 million views per month."[25] The blog, currently owned by NaturallyCurly.com, provides a platform where Black women can communication hardships and journeys of coming into their self-acceptance.

Vlogger Taren Guy, who now uses the handle Lucid LivingTV, has transitioned her YouTube channel from one focusing on natural hair to one featuring her freeform locs and journey through discovery. Such transformations in demonstrate womanist sensibilities that are focused not just on the politics of Black hair but also on the overall empowerment and vitality of Black women.[26] YouTubers like Lucid LivingTV also discuss the unfortunate backlash across the natural hair community when virtual and real lives collide.

"2 Sisters | 1 Mission: Curating Naturalista Chic," Natural Hair Does Care is a multiplatform brand with more than 3,000 subscribers on YouTube, 25,544 friends on Facebook, and 243,000 followers and 15,815 posts on Instagram. The creators' Instagram handle @NATURALHAIRDOESCARE was inspired by the saying "long hair, don't care," which is said to have originated in the white hippie community in the 1960s. That slogan was reborn into pop culture in 2009 and trickled down into the Black community.[27] It suggests that those with long, flawless, straight hair have a wonderful and carefree life. Natural Hair Does Care counters that concept and works to empower Black women with natural hair—which is seen as less attractive because of its seemingly short length, which appears short a direct result of its kinky, coily biology.

Team Natural, like many social media influencers, is a multiplatform brand that exists on Facebook, Twitter, Pinterest, and Instagram. The brand has its largest platform via Instagram, with over 505,000 followers. @Teamnatural_'s Instagram profile promotes the claim that natural hair is not a fad but a movement. The page is an album of the virtual natural hair movement, featuring Black women who proudly wear their hair in its natural state. Each post features images of other Instagram personalities and captions of empowerment and strength while promoting a positive self-image and high levels of self-esteem.

Instagram hashtags like #melaninpoppin and #blackgirlmagic affirm Black women's beauty and vitality. Although these hashtags are not synonymous with #TeamNatural or the natural hair community, they illustrate how perceptions of Black beauty have expanded to include natural hair, straight hair, and hair extensions. In this way, Instagram appears to be a site that advocates the idea that so-called good hair is ultimately any hairstyle that makes Black women happy.

FORUMS FOR BLACK HAIR CARE

Online platforms have become critical forums for Black hair care, allowing different threads of discussion, advocacy, and information-sharing about Black hair. Forums are created in several ways: for example, members register to participate on independently run Black hair sites, while broader social networks can very easily accommodate users from various interests and expectations. On all platforms, users can create posts with still and moving inspirational images that highlight ideal hairstyles, reviews of natural hair products and salon services, and tips on styling natural hair on children.

The discursive nature of blogging includes spaces for comments, which allows blog sites and microblogs, like the comment sections of YouTube and Instagram, to become spaces for democratizing views and political commentary. Visitor comments on these platforms reveal knowledge that exposes the varying opinions inside and outside the natural hair community. The natural hair community is a complex web of different ideas and approaches to being natural, which changes across gender, racial, ethnicity, class, sexual, and geographical lines.

The comment and forum sections on websites and blogs, YouTube, and Instagram are spaces where diverse perspectives within the natural hair movement come to life. The voices are affirming in some instances and oppositional in others. As the natural hair movement became affirmed inside and outside of mainstream virtual spaces, specific rules of ownership and natural hair practice became apparent, including who can be a part of #TeamNatural and what hair textures and styling methods fit in the natural hair category.

The website Nappturality.com provides a forum for discussions regarding natural hair. forum members can create posts with inspirational images of their ideal hairstyles, reviews of natural hair products and salon services, and tips on styling children's natural hair. As on most websites with profile-based systems, members must register and log in to access Nappturality's forums and blog content. Members can post on discussion forums and blogs on various topics from hair to fashion and wellness that contribute content to the site.[28]

USER DESIGN THAT DICTATES VIRTUAL ACCESS

User design considers the case with which web users can navigate, discover, and ultimately find information. Natural hair websites and blogs, YouTube, and Instagram, have varying levels of user design complexity that dictate their ease of use. One could assume the reason for this complexity is the interactive design that curates the user's website experience. In some instances, the interactive designs for highly brand-oriented websites or blogs can have more complex navigation maps, directing users to more access points that require understanding how to engage with content. However, website designs with clearer navigation feel more intuitive; these include carefully curated blogging categories and dropdowns that help users understand the kinds of content they can explored under various topics.

Nappturality.com is not the easiest site to navigate, nor is its design particularly intuitive. The site content is interwoven through different portals and access points across, and it will take some users time to find certain kinds of content. Additionally, the site includes banner ads that do not connect to the site's content and have several inconsistencies with the design. Nonetheless, the site provides an opportunity to connect Black women, via profiles that document their natural hair journeys and forums and other content that connects them with other women engaging in the same activity.

DIGITAL STORYTELLING

Where the nuances among the natural hair community on blogs are expressed primarily through text-based activism, other social media platforms present Black women with new audiovisual methods for digital storytelling and expression. While blogs often include links to photographs and audiovisual content, sites like YouTube and Instagram create platforms that place visually stimulating discourse at the center. The move from written to visual communication offers Black women new avenues for narrating their experiences, from multimedia editorial content to photographic and video stories. In this way, the virtual natural hair community gives Black women specific visual tools that allow them to tell their unique stories of natural hair in their own way, similar to the approaches of traditional film, video, and television.

Additionally, social media platforms effective tools for marketing and for sharing new ideas. The collective use of photography, short videos, and brief stories provides an instant marketing platform to communicate ideas that can reach a massive public the way mass communications use commercials. Instagram provides especially gratifying visual experiences and is more impactful and less distracting than other social networking platforms requiring more time to analyze. Instagram allows Black women to speak to other Black women through images and brief videos that they can easily comment on and scroll through. Instagram stories, in particular, allow Black women content creators to post even shorter narratives that cater to wider audiences. For example, Naptura185's brand is not only limited to YouTube; rather, she tells stories through her blog, and Twitter, Facebook, and Instagram accounts. She also vlogs about her personal life, family, beauty, and other lifestyle interests on her other YouTube accounts, @DearNaptura185 and @WhitneyWhite.

CONCLUSION

A visual analysis of various natural hair blogs and websites and social media platforms provides a description and narrative of how the virtual natural hair movement has changed over time. These platforms celebrate Black beauty in various forms, providing room for multiple interpretations. Websites and macro blogs like Nappturality.com and CurlyNikki.com still exist, despite the constant change in digital real estate. While early websites focused on text-centered content on forums and blogs, new trends within digital media have opened the door for mainstream social media platforms. YouTube and Instagram offer Black women new visual methods to show the world how vital natural hairstyling is and how it should be accepted in the dominant culture. Likewise, the increased use of pictures and moving images in the design of websites and blogs shows how effective and interchangeable images are in empowering others.

Visual representations of Black women online promoting natural hair care have significantly affected how women with natural hair are perceived. In the United States and abroad, Black women can see through virtual spaces why representation matters and how digital media affects everyday decisions. While much more can be studies, a visual analysis of social media platforms helps define the specific ways social media transforms perceptions over time. Furthermore, an analysis of various digital tools used to promote natural hair online provides a unique understanding of technology and its impact on the education and empowerment of Black women. Social media has given Black women a space to affirm natural forms of Black beauty that needed to be reclaimed. In her essay "In Search of My Mother's Gardens," Alice Walker encourages us to look high and low for spaces where Black women express their creativity every day. We can look at what the natural hair movement in virtual space has become after its almost twenty-year existence. In essence, the natural hair community is a garden in full bloom—a celebration of Black beauty online—allowing Black women to see their virtue. Compellingly, the natural hair movement online allows Black women to take to Alice Walker's words to heart: "Guided by my heritage of a love of beauty and a respect for strength—in search of my mother's gardens, I found my own."[29]

NOTES

1. Lauren Cross, "Mothers-for-Natural-Hair: The Afro-Cyberella's Social Media Guide to Afrocentric Hair," in *Mothering and Literacies*, ed. Linda Shuford Evans and Amanda Richey (Bradford, ON: Demeter Press, 2013), 221–36; Nancy Hafkin and Sophia Huyer, introduction to *Cinderella or Cyberella? Empowering Women in the Knowledge Society*, ed. Nancy Hafkin and Sophia Huyer (Sterling, VA: Kumarian Press, 2006), 1.

2. "The New Frontier: Black Women and Tech Activism," *African American Policy Forum*, accessed Sept. 30, 2019, https://www.aapf.org/hdd-2017; Erika Jefferson, "Where Are the Black Women in STEM Leadership?," *Scientific American* (blog), Apr. 23, 2019, https://blogs.scientificamerican.com/voices/where-are -the-black-women-in-stem-leadership/.

3. Latoya Lee, "Virtual Homeplace: (Re)Constructing the Body through Social Media," in *Women of Color and Social Media Multitasking: Blogs, Timelines, Feeds, and Community*, ed. Keisha Edwards Tassie and Sonja M. Brown Givens (Lanham, MD: Lexington, 2015), 92–93.

4. Tameka N. Ellington, "Social Networking Sites: A Support System for African-American Women Wearing Natural Hair," *International Journal of Fashion Design, Technology and Education* 8, no. 1 (2014): 21–29.

5. Tiffany Gill, "#TeamNatural: Black Hair and The Politics of Community in Digital Media," *Journal of Contemporary African Art* 37 (2015): 75.

6. Gill, "#TeamNatural," 75.

7. Douglas Kellner and Gooyong Kim, "YouTube, Critical Pedagogy, and Media Activism," *Education Pedagogy and Cultural Studies* 32, no. 1 (2010): 8.

8. Theresa Senft, *Camgirls: Celebrity and Community in the Age of Social Networks* (New York: Peter Lang, 2008).

9. Jamila Bey, "'Going Natural' Requires Lots of Help," *New York Times*, June 8, 2011.

10. Gill, "#TeamNatural," 73, 74.

11. Tiffany Gill, *Beauty Shop Politics: African American Women's Activism in the Beauty Industry* (Champaign: Univ. of Illinois Press, 2010).

12. Gill, "#TeamNatural," 75.

13. Gill, "#TeamNatural," 75.

14. Ellington, "Social Networking Sites," 22.

15. Cheryl Thompson, "Black Women, Beauty, and Hair as a Matter of Being," *Women's Studies* 38, no. 8 (2009): 835–36, 852.

16. Noliwe M. Rooks, "Wearing Your Hair Wrong: Hair, Drama, and a Polities of Representation for African American Women at Play on a Battlefield," in *Recovering the Black Female Body: Self Representations by African American Women,* ed. Michael Bennet and Vanessa D. Dickerson (New Brunswick, NJ: Rutgers Univ. Press, 2001).

17. Lisa Nakamura, *Cybertypes: Race, Ethnicity, and Identity on the Internet* (New York: Routledge, 2002).

18. Shauntae Brown White, "Releasing the Pursuit of Bouncin' and Behavin' Hair: Natural Hair as An Afrocentric Feminist Aesthetic for Beauty," *International Journal of Media and Cultural Politics* 1, no. 3 (2005): 295–308. Black feminist scholar Patricia Hill Collins speaks to the complementary nature of applying Afrocentricity with feminism to describe the experiences of Black women in *Black Feminist Thought: Knowledge, Consciousness and the Politics of Empowerment,* 2nd ed. (New York: Routledge, Taylor & Francis, 2000). In an exploration on the state of Black feminism, B. Belaineh writes about the need to expand the African woman's standpoint in Black feminism in her article "AfroCentricity, Sisterhood, and African Feminisms: An African Woman's Standpoint in Black Feminist Thought," *Medium,* Apr. 14, 2016, https://medium.com/black-feminist-thought-2016/afrocentricity-sisterhood-and-african-feminisms-an-african-woman-s-standpoint-in-black-feminist-2fe42cf31f62.

19. White, "Releasing the Pursuit," 295, 296, 299. White asserts that African American women who choose to wear their hair natural are making a rhetorical statement to resist Eurocentric hair ideals and accepting Afrocentric beauty standards, which may be contrary to public and political standards.

20. Alice Walker, "Oppressed Hair Puts a Ceiling on the Brain," *Living by The Word: Selected Writings 1973–1987* (Sept. 2013), https://alicewalkersgarden.com/2013/09/oppressed-hair-puts-a-ceiling-on-the-brain/.

21. Lauren Cross, "It's Just Hair: African American Women, Womanist Agency, and Natural Hair Blogs," presentation, annual meeting of the National Women's Studies Association, Atlanta, GA, Nov. 10, 2011.

22. Janice Hamlet, "Assessing Womanist Thought: The Rhetoric of Susan L. Taylor," in *The Womanist Reader,* ed. Layli Phillips (New York: Routledge, 2006), 223.

23. Layli Phillips, introduction to Phillips, *Womanist Reader,* xi.

24. Alice Walker, "In Search of My Mother's Gardens," in *In Search of Our Mothers' Gardens: Womanist Prose* (New York: Harcourt Brace Jovanovich, 1983).

25. Lee, "Virtual Homeplace," 78.

26. Layli Maparyan, *The Womanist Idea* (New York: Routledge, 2012).

27. Meirav Devash, "Where Does the Phrase 'Long Hair Don't Care' Come From, Anyway?," *Town & Country,* Apr. 25, 2016, https://www.townandcountrymag.com/society/news/a5946/long-hair-dont-care/.

28. Gill, "#TeamNatural," 74.

29. Alice Walker, "In Search of Our Mothers' Gardens," in *Within the Circle: An Anthology of African American Literacy Criticism from the Harlem Renaissance to the Present,* ed. Angelyn Mitchell (Durham, NC: Duke Univ. Press, 1994), 409.

CHAPTER 9

Project Naptural

A SOCIOCULTURAL INITIATIVE FOR NAPTURAL LIVING

*Creating Space to Educate, Connect, and Empower
Black Women through the Project Naptural Initiative*

Terresa Moses

The field of design research has been moving toward academics and industry professionals asking critical questions about how design affects users' experiences. As a design researcher, the author has centered this work around the intersectional experiences of Black women who have chosen to wear their hair in its naturally curly, kinky, Afro-textured state—naptural (nappy + natural). The study will examine how white supremacist culture influences today's Eurocentric beauty standards and negatively affects the choices Black women believe they have regarding styling their naptural hair. The data will then reveal how design and design research can help improve the experiences of Black naptural women by creating culturally accessible spaces that allow education, connection, and empowerment.

THE NATURAL HAIR JOURNEY

The process by which a Black woman chooses to wear her hair in its natural state—without using harmful chemical relaxers—is called her *natural hair journey*. This journey involves a variety of experiences that discourage or support her hair choice. Using the ecological systems theory developed by Urie Bronfenbrenner, the author analyzed her hair choices to understand better how culture, media, and interpersonal relationships affected her hair choices.[1] During this analysis, the author discovered that her hair choices were deeply connected to those of her older siblings and friends. These relationships were heavily influenced by mass media and how society and culture valued beauty. For instance, around 2008, many of the author's friends and colleagues decided to wear their hair in its naptural state. The author was not used to seeing her hair this way, and the Black women in the mass media were not embracing their naptural hair, which influenced her to continue chemically relaxing her hair. At one point when friends were trying to help her understand the benefits of naptural hair, the author ignorantly replied, "I'm sorry, but natural hair is ugly. I need mine to blow in the wind." This story is disheartening because of how often it is told by Black women when speaking about their natural hair journey.

Negative self-perceptions about one's naptural hair are directly centered around intersectionality—being Black and being a woman.[2] Kimberlé Crenshaw first introduced the theory of intersectionality in reference to the intersecting marginalizing experiences Black women face. Crenshaw addresses how both antiracism and feminism have left "women of colour invisible in plain sight."[3] The author argues that this is true in every area of society, particularly within the beauty industry, even though Black women are the largest consumers of hair and beauty products.[4] The juxtaposition between this and having the least amount of representation in advertisements, marketing, and product availability is a constant reminder to Black women that they do not matter and should not be seen.

So how can an industry in a capitalist society ignore its greatest consumer? This results directly results from white supremacy. This form of injustice, at its core, works to remove opportunities and representation from people of color. While some doubt the existence of white supremacist culture, its prevalence, and its violent nature show up in the beauty industry, perpetuating the erasure of Black womanhood.[5] White supremacy creates a system that values, represents, and defends whiteness and white beauty standards at every turn. This toxic culture makes it almost impossible for society to see the beauty in Black women, let alone value their existence.

For example, the lack of access to mainstream products suited to care for Black naptural hair within hotels supports white supremacy. The anxiety around hair for a Black woman, especially as she plans a trip, increases the closer she gets to her travel date, almost always with the question "What are you going to do with your hair?" As a result of white supremacy monopolizing the beauty industry, the complementary skin and hair products at hotels are only suited for the white population. This reality has never been questioned openly by the public until recently, when Grammy-nominated singer-songwriter Halsey sparked a public debate via Twitter.[6] Defenders of the white supremacist culture called for her to "purchase her own products" and stated that "shampoo can't be racist," when, in fact, the beauty industry and the dominant US society are linked to institutional racism. Black women are hindered in their natural hair journeys because they must constantly inhabit spaces that do not allow them to bring their full identities to the table or feel supported.

The lack of education and awareness around these topics not only negatively affects the natural hair journeys of Black women but perpetuates the normalcy of whiteness as the standard of beauty and being. White people are not exposed to the experiences of Black women; they do not understand that naptural hair requires different products, styles, and processes. This lack of cultural awareness causes hair discrimination in the workplace, the embarrassment of Black girls in educational environments, and the absence of naptural hair products from mainstream retail stores. Education and exposure are necessary not only for Black women with naptural hair to live full lives but for the full integration of Black womanhood within the mainstream culture, to stop the harm caused by white supremacy.

Hair is such a defining and sacred feature for Black women—physically, emotionally, and spiritually—that the threat of white supremacy negatively affects the choices surrounding it. Discrimination and the racial gaze are so strong that Black women would rather revert to using harmful chemical relaxers to straighten their hair in hopes of assimilation than learn how to care for their naptural curls. Understanding the need for change and a space dedicated to these experiences, the author used design research methods to create a sociocultural initiative for naptural living, Project Naptural.

WHAT IS PROJECT NAPTURAL?

Project Naptural is the result of a design research thesis examining how design and design research might assist in overcoming the negative perceptions Black women come to know about their naturally Afro-textured hair.[7] These perceptions are ultimately tied to self-identity and developed from interpersonal relationships affected by media heavily influenced by white supremacist culture. The burden placed on Black women does not allow room for error or imperfection, pressuring Black women to choose straighter hairstyles, similar to their white counterparts. Consider Michelle Obama, who is no longer serving as the First Lady and now feels free to wear her naptural curls in public.[8] Project Naptural exists to overcome these harmful perceptions through education, connection, and the empowerment of Black women with naptural hair. Since 2015, the question that continues to guide the author's work through this initiative is this: What type of interactive educational tool might most effectively enlighten Black women about what is available to them regarding the manipulation of their naptural hair and its effects on how they and others perceive them?

METHODS

To further contextualize the naptural hair phenomenon, anthropological research methods were employed, to help understand the culture and life experiences of Black women with naptural hair.[9] A triangulation research method included interviews, focus groups, observations, and the analysis of comments left on graffiti walls. Using these methods—supported by grounded theory, ecological systems theory, critical theory, and phenomenology—helped to reveal the themes of Black women's experiences. From this data, a design approach was created with the aim of helping improve the self-perceptions of Black naptural women.

Each of the fifteen Black naptural women interviewed spoke negatively about the beginning of her hair journey. They mentioned parents or family members determined to straighten their curls who burned their scalps with the hot comb or a chemical relaxer. They spoke about special occasions when their hair would be "done up" or "fixed" to be presentable. Consistently, many thought their hair was never good enough.

Using a semi-structured questionnaire, the interviews started with a simple question, "What are some childhood hair experiences that you can tell me about?" Participant Juanita responded:

> You know, my mom used to joke about the "kitchen," you know, trying to get the "kitchen." She used to comb it . . . because my hair does not really have a loose curl. It sort of naps up, so she always used to call my hair. . . ."I gotta get the Kuntas out" you know like Kunta Kinte [laughs]. She would be like, "Come here, we gotta get the Kuntas out" [laughs]. Get the naps out you know.

Their families perpetuated society's notion of beautiful as straight and long hair. Heuristically, the researcher remembers her own family critiquing the texture of her sister's hair and darker complexion. Additionally, many women mentioned discrimination in the workplace. One woman commented particularly on how her choice to go natural prevented her from a promotion. The woman, who worked in a hair salon, was told by administration: "We are concerned because you would be the face of the administration.

Because the white supremist culture has been perpetuated throughout society and culture, many women hesitate to embrace their naptural curls. Many Black naptural women struggled internally for a long time, even years,

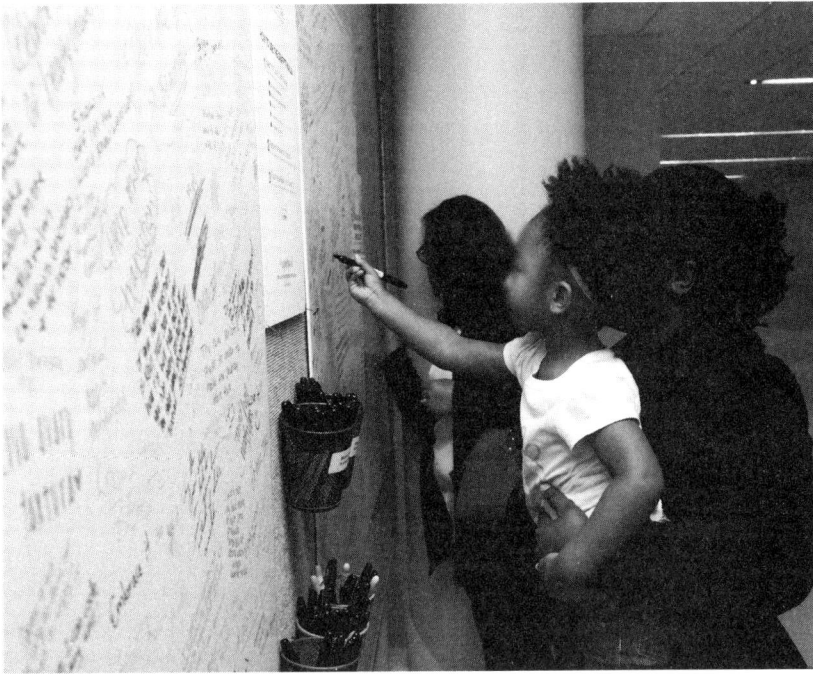

FIG. 1. Woman and child responding to graffiti wall prompt, 2016 (Photo courtesy of Jen Sulak)

before deciding their physical and emotional health was at stake. Cultural factors, family influence, and even sexual identity all play roles in the decision to go natural. Natural hair has been said to be less feminine. Those who decide to either transition or do the big chop make that choice because of health concerns, self-acceptance, or as a means of empowering children to accept themselves.[10] Of the 211 women who responded to the question on the graffiti walls: "What do you love about your naptural hair?" 18 percent said that they loved their naptural hair because of its versatility (Fig. 1). Seeing that both shared experiences and natural hair's versatility contributed to positive natural hair experiences, the author was determined to find a way that these factors could be visually displayed. She hypothesized that the visualization of the graffiti wall could prompt connections between Black women and educate them about what naptural hair can offer.

RESULTS

Hair-itage Poster Series and Exhibition

Based on the findings, a series of thirty posters was designed that supported versatility, highlighted similar and relatable experiences, and represented the beauty of naptural hair. The posters display the many styles that can be created with naptural hair. Each poster includes an illustration of a Black

THE HIGH PUFF

THE CORN ROWS

THE PONY HAWK

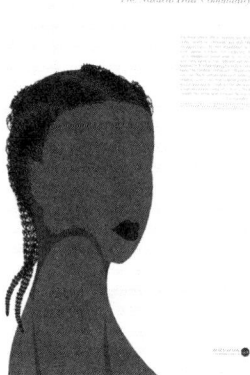

FIGS. 2–4.
Project
Naptural digital
illustrations
of hairstyles
using natural
elements such
as feathers,
leaves, and
flower petals
(2005–2017).
These images
represent the
beauty and
creativity of
natural hair.

naptural woman or girl from the shoulders up. The dimensions of the poster, 24.7 x 40 inches, are equal to the golden section, using the golden ratio, said to be the epitome of beauty within design. The illustrations filled most of each posters, evoking dominance in the hierarchy. There are hundreds of hair textures within the Black community; therefore, the hair textures in the illustration were created to reflect textures found in the environment. The first set of twelve posters is illustrated with feathers (Fig. 2), the second set of twelve posters with leaves (Fig. 3), and the final set, six posters, with flower petals (Fig. 4). Each poster includes a quote from an interviewee, an excerpt about cultural appropriation, statistics based on primary research from interviews, or a combination of the three.

The first time the illustrations were exhibited, the attendees reacted with, in a word, awe. Participants from various backgrounds engaged with the artwork and the prompted interactive pieces connected with the work. Many Black women hugged the author during the exhibition opening and expressed their gratitude. One woman, with tears in her eyes, said how important she felt because not only could she see herself on the walls, but academia accepted her experiences as valid—valid enough to do a whole thesis. Project Naptural's goal was to continue empowering women to go natural and stay natural, regardless of societal pressure to conform to dominant beauty standards. Participant responses showed that the project had the potential to do just that.

As the author continued to work on the expansion of Project Naptural, she explored supporting the exhibition with learning opportunities and intentional conversation. After the 2016 exhibition, the author moved from Dallas, Texas, to Duluth, Minnesota. She found that the need for Project Naptural was even greater in an area with little to no support for communities of color and deeply rooted racism that expands the racial divide and hosts some of the worst racial disparities in the nation.[11] Duluth is 92 percent white, which results in the toxicity of white supremacy prevailing. Another element she realized while engaging in the naptural hair community is the large population of mixed-race families and transracial adoptees seeking support and connectivity around their identity and naptural hair practices. These additional factors prompted her to create spaces that center on the experiences of Black naptural women in addition to educating white allies so they can participate, learn, and grow as well.

A $10,000 University of Minnesota's Imagine Fund Special Events Grant and a $1,500 grant from the Northland Foundation were used to support the Project Naptural workshops and symposiums. The grants allowed the author to provide stipends to facilitators, guest speakers, panelists, and photographers—all of whom were Black women. They also allowed for the purchase of naptural-haired mannequin heads for demos, hairstyling tools; products for giveaways and demos; bus passes for attendees; and printing of the last set of illustrated posters, workbooks, and programs.

2018 Workshops

The workshops were created as a resource for the community of curly, kinky, and Afro-textured female-identified individuals. They took place over three months, with an emphasis on information sharing and dissemination to help educate, empower, and connect individuals with naptural hair. The workshops were free to attend, although registration was required. Thirty-six participants, with ages ranging from seven to fifty-two, attended. Each workshop lasted two hours and was held from 4:00 to 6:00 P.M.

The workshops were held at the Duluth Public Library's Green Room. It was important that they be accessible to bus lines and centrally located. The workshops included sessions on historical breakdowns, culture contextualizing, hairstyling demos, personal and visual journaling, and product-making demos, as well as discussions with participants. The author employed Sandra Oyinloye as a cofacilitator. With her background in sociology, youth advocacy, and hair braiding, she was able to help guide discussion and facilitate active learning experiences. Sandra also served as an active partner in planning the workshop schedules.

A workbook designed to facilitate the dissemination of information for all learning styles was given out during the workshop. The workbook allowed space for participants to visually journal and provided line drawings that participants could color in (Fig. 5). The workbook was an essential part of the workshops; it helped participants understand the mission of Project

Naptural, allowed for visual journaling and notes, and helped guide discussion. The workbooks were passed out at the beginning of each workshop and collected at the end of each day. On the final day, participants could keep their workbooks. This was a great way to encourage attendance and participation. Also, each day, a slide presentation was designed to correlate with the workbook pages to help participants stay on track.

Workshop Day 1: The Roots

The first workshop, "The Roots: Foundations of Natural Hair," introduced Project Naptural and then introduced the participants to each other. Within the workbook, the author and the workshop participants also reviewed the natural hair community's language, with a "Naptural Index," at the back of the workbook, created by the researcher, which included words like *beady-beads, kitchen,* and *tender-headed.*[12] Participants also discussed a breakdown of Andre Walker's original hair typing system, to help attendees "better understand their hair texture" (Fig. 5).[13] Helping participants understand their texture enabled them to better care for their hair. A section on hair care was included in the index, which explored trimming and washing techniques and styling options. The last section of the index included texture changing or modification, including, for example, terms like *relaxer, stretching,* and *texturizer.* Relaxers and texturizers are chemical hair straighteners that make extremely kinky hair straight. The act of "stretching" the hair, which originates in West Africa, can be done via various techniques, such as wrapping thread around the hair or twisting the hair while wet, and untwisting it after it dries.

FIG. 5.
Participants'
engaged
workbooks—
indexes and
hair tutorial
pages

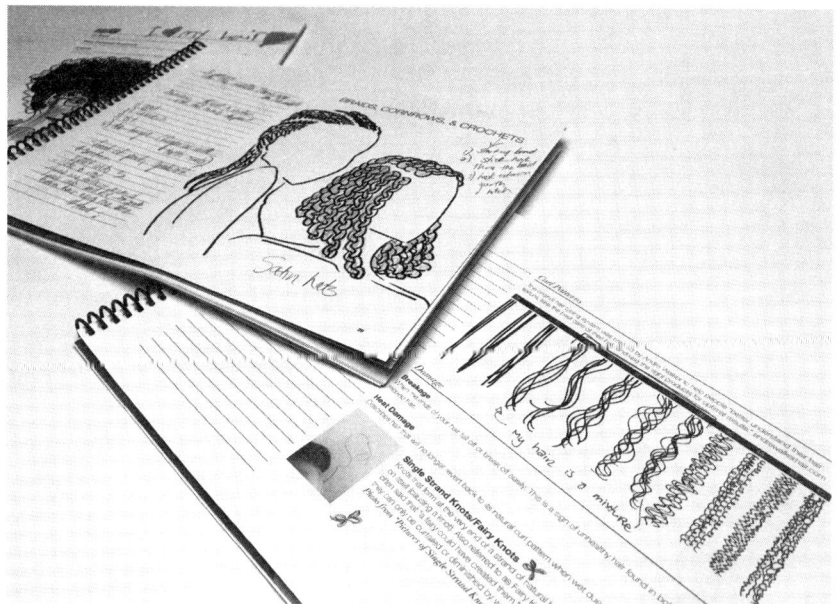

The section on texture changing in led seamlessly to our next topic, "The Science of Natural Hair," which explained that because the traditions and hair culture of Africa were stolen from Black people during slavery, a "cure" was implemented to rid them of their nappy, wooly hair, in hopes of assimilation. Hair was first "cured" with concoctions like axle grease or the combination of butter and a hot knife run through the hair (comparable to the modern flat iron). The harshest concoction for straightening the hair was lye, a chemical compound made popular by Garrett Augustus Morgan in the 1900s. Despite its harmfulness, the compound still exists in today' chemical relaxers. Chemical relaxers lead to serious damage to hair:

- chemical burns, leaving bald areas on the scalp where the hair might never grow back
- breakage and unhealthy or damaged hair
- hair breakage resulting from at-home kits being used without proper application
- correlation with fibroid tumors[14]
- unhealthy lifestyles related to not exercising due to fear of hair reverting to its natural state.

The day's last topic was "The Psychology of Natural Hair." During this time, attendees and facilitators discussed how the psychologist Cheryl Thompson of the University of Michigan focuses on the historical issues of natural hair and how she tells many different stories about Black women and their constant battle with naptural hair.[15] Thompson uses interviews and conversations about hair to discuss how media and social interactive processes mediate one's grooming choices while simultaneously ascribing an aesthetic value to one's body. However, value is assigned to Black hair, whether by family, the Black community, mainstream media influences, or historical traumas. This value even brings up the age-old argument in Black culture: good hair versus bad hair.

A mainstream example of struggles within the Black hair community was brought to the forefront in Chris Rock's documentary *Good Hair*, which includes interviews, focus groups, and data analysis of Black women and their hair.[16] Rock's study began when his young daughter asked him, "Why don't I have good hair?" The mentality around natural hair is learned and starts at a very young age, and society is trained to undervalue Black naptural hair, skin tones, features, and the very essence of Black womanhood.

The first day ended with a "Find It!" activity to help participants learn the Naptural Hair index. Participants were divided into two groups, with each given sticky notes to place on the large illustrations. They were given a list of terms and tasked with finding words that would be classified into one of three categories: Hair Textures, Hairstyles, and Hair Terms. The group that correctly identified all of them first won a copy of the natural hair illustrated posters created by the author.

Workshop Day 2

The second-day workshop, "HAIRitage: The Historical Contexts of Natural Hair," introduced the phases of adaptation as a way of framing the historical experiences of Black women. It was explained that after the Civil War and the emancipation of Black people, an intracultural or intraracial divide was created in the Black community due to identifiers such as skin color, hair texture, and education level. As more Blacks were freed, they had access to a new world—unfamiliar and even scary at times. This was an "emotional refugee experience," writes Maggie O'Neill when describing global refugees and the transformative role of art.[17] The methodologies for sociocultural research in this field are defined by four phases.

Phase One is *Confusion,* shown by the period in Black beauty between 1865 and 1900. Feelings of confusion were met with the guilt of abandoning those at home who were perhaps still enslaved, mixed with a sense of relief of having escaped the dangers of slavery. Workshop participants learned about the domestication of slavery, the independence of freedom, and the ways enslaved Black women wore wigs and head scarves to achieve the white standard of beauty.

Phase Two is *Disillusion.* This period was between 1900 and 1959, during which time Black people experienced disillusionment as their expectations and hopes of freedom were not being met. It would take years for the United States to give Blacks what seemed "equal" opportunity, thus making clear why Black people would do everything in their power to become more like whites, freer. This period is reflected in the hair products that were invented to aid in assimilation, such as straighteners and chemical relaxers.

Phase Three is *Isolation.* The freed Black refugee experience from the 1960s through the 1990s, is defined by problems that may have been exacerbated by the emotional anxieties stemming from the inaccessibility of opportunities, social status, and political participation. Although Black people did everything they could to "belong," the fight for civil rights persisted. Among the various ways Black people identified themselves in the fight for freedom, many around the country would style their hair in its naturally Afro-textured state. This hairstyle, iconic to Black liberation, was synonymous with rebelling against the mainstream definition of beauty.

Phase Four is *Adaptation.* In the refugee experience, the adaptation phase takes years, depending on age, language, culture, gender, and whether one is alone or part of a family. This phase began in the 1990s and can extend two or three generations (if not more, with historical traumas). Workshop attendees discussed how Black women participating in the natural hair movement do so not out of rebellion but from a newfound acceptance of who they are while living in a culture dominated by whiteness. Black women throughout the United States are battling beauty standards and declaring their naptural selves beautiful.

The setup of the phases within the emotional refugee experience was a great way to introduce the activity for the day. The author shared her hair story using ecological theory, which guided participants on the journey to creating their own. The second-day workshop ended with a mix-and-match activity with posted photos of traditional West African hairstyles. The participants placed tags with the meanings of the styles (supplied by the author and her team) on top of the images they thought it fit best. For example, participants were to guess the meaning of the style in an image featuring a young girl from the Wolof culture of Senegal. We did this activity to help participants understand the historical significance of Black hairstyles.

Workshop Day 3

The third workshop, "Strands In, Stand Out: Braiding Styles and Protective Styling," centered on hair styling and demonstrations. The group created styles illustrated in the workbook. Space was provided next to the drawing for participants to write notes on how to best do the styles. They created four styles: first, finger coils and coil-outs; second, Bantu knots and Bantu knot-outs; third, two-strand twists and twist-outs; and fourth, braids, cornrows, and crochet styles. Participants worked together using step-by-step instructions to produce the styles, ensuring no one fell behind.

Styles were created on mannequin heads, which were described as having Afro-textured hair (Figs. 6 and 7). It was very difficult to find these

FIG. 6. Participants styling hair on mannequin heads

FIG. 7.
Participants
styling hair on
mannequin
heads

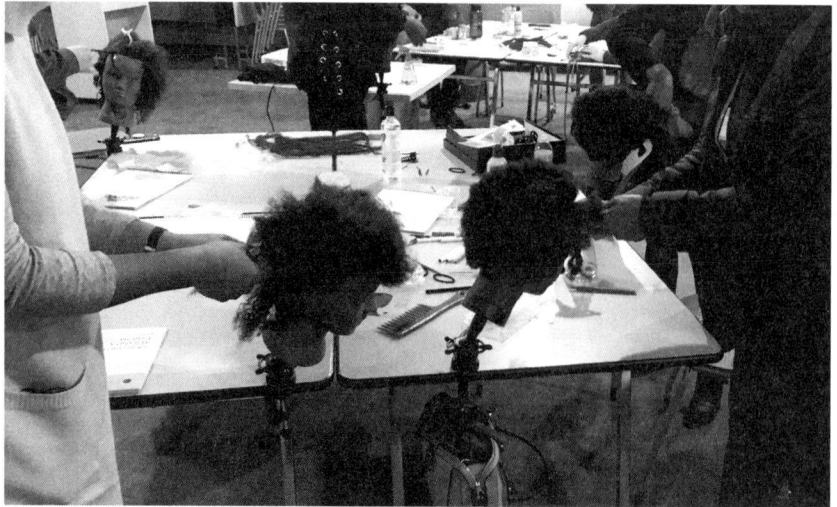

mannequin heads, and the author had to order from several places due to the lack of availability—a further example of Black beauty is ignored in the White supremacist mainstream. That internalized texture discrimination and colorism affected the workshop participants' experiences.

One young girl, in particular, felt this discrimination. Before starting the hair demos, each participant chose the mannequin head whose hair best matched their own hair texture. When a young girl chose a mannequin with a loose curl pattern, her mother directed her to a darker, more kinky, textured mannequin head. The young girl began to cry. As reflected in her response to the doll, she believed her own hair was ugly. For a few minutes, she denied that that was her texture, but after the cofacilitator explained how she loved this texture because it held styles very well, the young girl felt more at ease with choosing the mannequin that reflected her hair texture.

Workshop Day 4

The fourth workshop, "I'm Me and I'm Proud: Learning to Love Your Natural Hair," empowered participants through confidence-building exercises directly related to their hair and the community they had begun to build. At the beginning, they talked about stereotypes of natural hair in today's society, the term "nappy," and how many Black people overcame the stereotypes of "bad" hair. The workshop also addressed cultural appropriation, which helped participants understand that many cultural aspects around Black hair are often stolen and uncredited. As referenced in the workbook and on the Bantu knot illustration, a well-known white fashion designer, Marc Jacobs, culturally misappropriated Bantu knots. During his spring 2015 runway fashion show, Jacobs sent his models down the runway

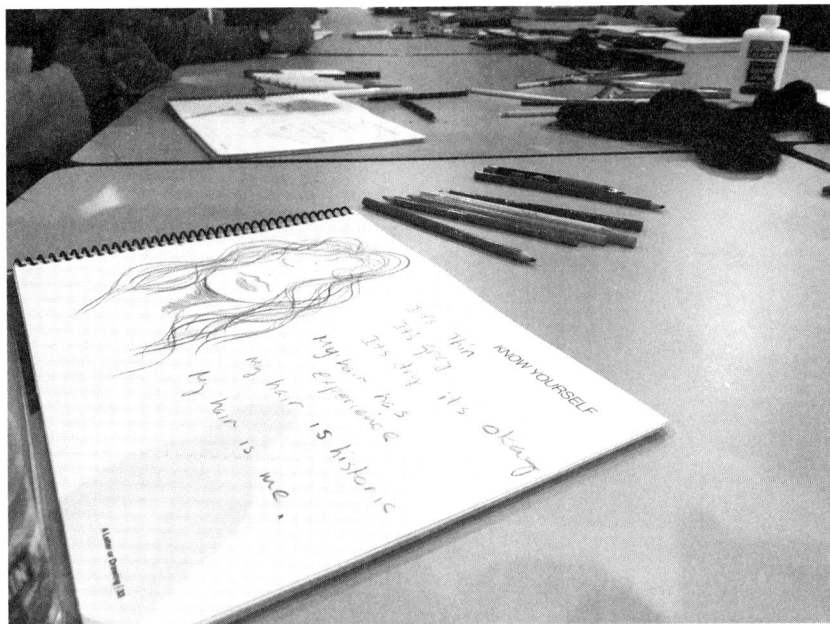

FIG. 8.
Participants'
written words
of affirmation

sporting Bantu knots down the centers of their heads. The hairstyle gained popularity with other white women, who claimed these were "mini-buns," and published hair tutorials crediting Jacobs for the style. This "sparked outrage among many Black women and men for linking the style to Marc Jacobs, rather than acknowledging its actual roots" in the Black community.[18] After the misappropriation, posts on Twitter and other social media platforms included photographs of Black women wearing Bantu knots with the hashtag #itaughtmarcjacobs.

After discussing some struggles navigating a white world as Black women, the group worked on an affirmation page (Fig. 8). They wrote empowering words that encouraged them and reminded them of the beauty they and their hair possessed. After this activity, the participants discussed the truths about natural hair. They talked about versatility, health, shrinkage, and appeal. Many participants brought up their own experiences of falling back in love with their roots during their own natural hair journeys.

The last activity of day four was sharing words of affirmation. Because individuals began to build relationships, they recognized admirable traits in each other that they could write on their "encourage others" pages. This sharing prompted discussions and community connections between participants. Then the group crafted self-portraits based on introspection and hair reflections (Fig. 9).

FIG. 9.
Participants'
self-portraits

Workshop Day 5

The fifth workshop, "Food for the 'Kitchen': Using and Making Natural Products," included product-making tutorials. It emphasized that natural products are healthy for natural hair and scalps. Participants also discussed the importance of using products that cleanse, moisturize, and seal in moisture to retain length and resist breakage.

Using a list of natural hair products from beautymunsta contributors, we had products available for participants to touch and use on their hair, including apple cider vinegar, coconut oil, honey, essential oils, shea butter, aloe vera, and African black soap. The group recreated four recipes supplied in the workbook from Chinwe of Hair and Health, including the African Black Soap Shampoo, Enhanced Shampoo, Whipped Shealoe, and Whipped Butter for Conditioner Lovers. A flaxseed hair gel recipe from Sointocurls was supplied, although it was not created during the workshop. Participants received containers they could store and take home after making the recipes.

Workshop Day 6

The final workshop, "Naptural Living: Lifestyle Changes for Naptural Living and Empowerment," focused on participants' next steps in the natural hair journey. The purpose of this session was to leave women feeling inspired and empowered to use the information they had gathered during the workshops. Spaces that allow for this type of community help overcome feelings of alienation and lack of self-confidence influenced by societal norms that perpetuate a lack of belonging in the beauty industry and professional environments.

YouTube channels by vloggers MahoganyCurls, MyNaturalSistas, and MoKnowsHair were introduced to help participants stay educated. Well-known Black women with naptural hair (Angela Davis, Assata Shakur, Janelle Monáe, Solange, and Viola Davis) were named to inspire participants. Facilitators mentioned resources to help attendees stay empowered, like our upcoming symposium and *CRWN* magazine. This day was full of making connections and sharing ways other women continue to feel empowered in a world that does not reflect them. The workshop ended with empowering giveaways like Solange's CD *A Seat at the Table,* with its well-known song "Don't Touch My Hair," and copies of *Black Panther* movie. And, as promised, participants took their workbooks home.

2018 Symposium

To help educate on topics and issues relevant to the natural hair community, the Natural Hair Symposium included the Project Naptural art exhibition and events in the same space. The symposium included guest speakers and stylists, a hair show with youth and adult hair models, presentations on the historical context of natural hair, and product and styling demos. The symposium was held at the American Indian Community Housing Organization's Dr. Robert Powless Cultural Center, in Duluth, on three separate days: September 1, 6:00–9:00 P.M., September 15, 3:00–6:00 P.M., and September 29, 3:00–6:00 P.M. More than two hundred registrants attended over the three days. The art exhibition remained for the entire month.

Symposium Day 1

This first day of the symposium included the art and natural hair show. The exhibition revealed art inspired by the beauty of natural hair while showing the art of doing natural hair. Five hair stylists worked on the models' hair, twenty total, from the early morning until the show, applying final touches during the first hour after the exhibition doors opened. As attendees entered the space, they were given a program that included the symposium schedule, a glossary of naptural terms, and line illustrations to color. Attendees were then guided to the gallery space to view and participate in some of the art and to ask questions of the stylists while they completed the models' hair (Figures 10–13). The event ended with a giveaway of products to all participants and three pieces of art.

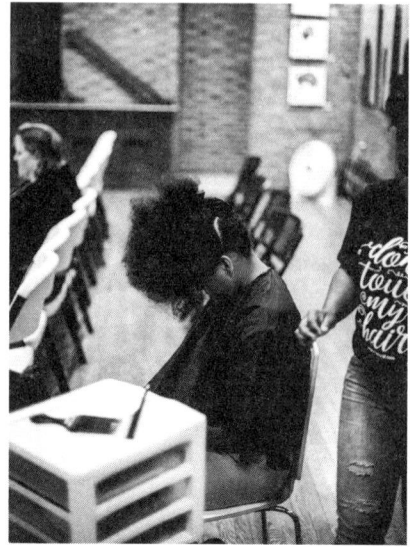

FIGS. 10–13. The Naptural Project Exhibition. (*top left*) The author's hair journey from childhood through adulthood. (Photos courtesy of Nemuel Nyangaresi)

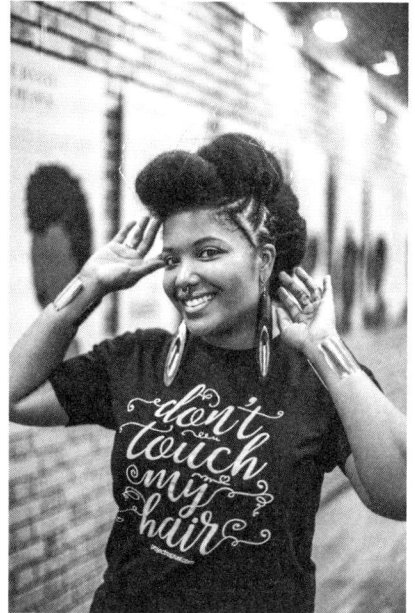

Symposium Day 2

The second day of the symposium focused on participants' hair stories. Attendees were seated at large tables to help facilitate discussion (Fig. 14). The day began with an explanation of the Project Naptural Initiative and its mission: to educate, empower, and connect (Fig. 15). Leading participants in dialogue discussed the history of natural hair and how their perceptions of how our past affects the present. Societal stigma and white supremacist culture's effect on our self-perception and hair was explained in length.

Next up was guest speaker Alex Steinman, who shared her hair journey, inspiring participants to discuss theirs. Steinman's natural hair journey has influenced her relationship with her children, giving them a sense of hair freedom she did not experience growing up. Then, participants worked on ecology, mapping out their hair journeys, and worked together to recall societal influences on their naptural hair perception. Before a break, attendees participated in a styling tutorial with scarves provided by the team as gifts.

The last activity of the day was hair tutorial demonstrations. Several hair mannequins were set up at each table, along with hair tools, like wide-toothed combs and bobby pins. The facilitators divided the symposium space into three station areas that attendees could explore Stretching Techniques—led by Jara McLarren—focusing on styles that stretch curls like Bantu knots, twists, twist outs, braids, braid outs, and flexi rods; Protective Styling—led

FIG. 14. Attendees of Symposium Day 2 seated at large tables (Photo courtesy of Hebron Girma)

FIG. 15. The author leading a discussion on the Project Naptural initiative (Photo courtesy of Hebron Girma)

by Sandra Oyinloye—focusing on cornrows, extensions, and crochet styles; and Styling Your Crown—led by the author—focusing on Afro puffs, fro-hawks, and the Afro. Attendees remained in their spots while the facilitators moved their stations around the room (Figs. 16–18). Group members spent thirty minutes at each station. At the end of the second day, a flat iron, hair products, and essential oils were given away, and each guest received a bag of gifts, along with another piece of hair art. Participants enjoyed learning about the different styling techniques and walking through their hair journeys.

Symposium Day 3

The last day of the symposium started with a panel of Black naptural women: Gabrielle Benton, psychologist; Salaam Witherspoon, community

FIG. 16. (*top*) and FIG. 17. (*below left*) Participants learning to cornrow (Photo courtesy of Hebron Girma)

FIG. 18. (*below right*) Jara McLarren teaching flexi rodding (Photo courtesy of Hebron Girma)

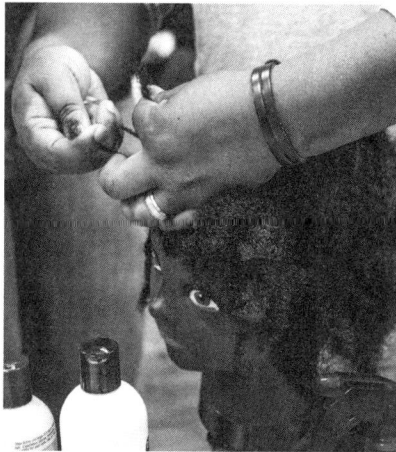

FIG. 19. The Symposium Day 3 panel (Photo courtesy of Hebron Girma)

organizer; NaTasha Lancour, youth advocate; Princess Kisob, director of equity and after-school programming, and Dr. Tina Opie, associate professor of management, who joined via Google Hangouts (Fig. 19). Afterward, attendees asked the panel members several questions:

1. Have you or when did you first chemically alter(ed) your curl pattern? What influenced your decision?
2. How long have you been natural, and did you have any fears when going natural?
3. What are some of your biggest influencers in wearing your natural hair?
4. Do you see a difference in yourself now compared to when you wore chemically altered hair?
5. Do others see a difference in you now compared to when you wore chemically altered hair?
6. Why do you think other women chose to or chose not to wear their hair natural?
7. How do you feel about mainstream/Eurocentric media appropriating Black hairstyles?

After the panel discussion and break, symposium attendees worked with the facilitators to produce hair products. Again, the facilitators worked in three stations to assist attendees in creating Whipped Butter, Whipped Shealoe, and Enhanced Shampoo and the attendees moved from table to table every half hour (Figs. 20–21). Containers were provided so attendees attendees could take home to use the new products (Figs. 23–24). The symposium ended with product and hair-tool giveaways, swag-bag fillers, and art giveaways. Attendees were also invited to join a Facebook group to stay in touch with their newfound community.

IMPLICATIONS

The Project Naptural initiative will continue with more interviews and focus groups with future attendees, specifically those living in the Minnesota northland, to assist in understanding the specific needs of Black women in this region. The next event is currently being planned to take place at the

FIGS. 20–21. (*right*) Facilitators leading the product-making demonstrations

FIGS. 22–23. (*below*) Participants making products (Photos courtesy of Hebron Girma)

Tweed Museum of Art in Duluth. This all-inclusive conference and symposium will be centered around Project Naptural's mission of education, connectivity, and empowerment.

This future symposium will continue the theme of representation and empowerment by including art from various Black women to represent the beauty of natural hair, in an exhibit at the Tweed. The opening will host a hair show in which women will walk through the entire space, heads lifted high. In partnership with the museum, we will display many of the African artifacts from the Tweed's collection, reflecting the historical importance of Black culture. Each attendee will register for one of four tracks or choose an à la carte option, that include the following: first, "The Business of Black Hair"—focusing on Black hair shops, naptural hair in the workplace, and professional development; second, "Hands-on Hair"—learning to style yourself, learning to style your dependent, braiding techniques, and product making; third, "Culture and Identity"—a deep dive into race, racism, cultural appropriation, and Black culture; and fourth, "Lifestyle and Healing"—focusing on mental health, empowerment, whole-body healing, exercise, and food. We will be partnering with the Duluth YWCA, whose mission is to eliminate racism and empower women. Registration fees for this conference will include lodging, meals, swag, and childcare, but not travel to and from the conference. The committee has already been formed, and the team is seeking grant funding and securing keynote speakers.

Project Naptural has positively affected the author's community, pushing her toward advocacy. Being a Black naptural woman in a white world is not easy, so the author encourages future researchers/designers to continue designing spaces to benefit those who need them most.

NOTES

1. Urie Bronfenbrenner, *The Ecology of Human Development: Experiments by Nature and Design* (Cambridge, MA: Harvard Univ. Press, 1979).
2. Kimberlé Crenshaw, "Demarginalizing the Intersection of Race and Sex: A Black Feminist Critique of Antidiscrimination Doctrine, Feminist Theory, and Antiracist Politics [1989]," *University of Chicago Legal Forum* 1989, no. 1 (2018): 139–67.
3. Bim Adewunmi, "Kimberlé Crenshaw on Intersectionality: 'I Wanted to Come up with an Everyday Metaphor That Anyone Could Use,'" *New Statesman America,* Apr. 2, 2014, https://www.newstatesman.com/lifestyle/2014/04/kimberl-crenshaw-intersectionality-i-wanted-come-everyday-metaphor-anyone-could.
4. "Resilient, Receptive and Relevant," *Nielsen,* Sept. 19, 2013, https://www.nielsen.com/us/en/insights/report/2013/resilient-receptive-and-relevant/.
5. Brian Stelter, "Tucker Carlson Wrongly Tells His Viewers the Country's White Supremacy Problem 'Is a Hoax,'" *CNN,* Aug. 7, 2019, https://www.cnn.com/2019/08/07/media/tucker-carlson-white-supremacy-reliable-sources/index.html.

6. Amber Ferguson, "Singer Halsey Stirs Debate over Hotels Offering Only 'White People Shampoo,'" *Washington Post,* Apr. 30, 2018.

7. Terresa Moses, "Project Naptural," *Project Naptural,* Nov. 17, 2014, https://terresa moses.com/port/projectnaptural/.

8. Jenna Amatulli, "Michelle Obama's Natural Curls Make Waves at Essence Fest," *HuffPost,* July 9, 2019, https://www.huffpost.com/entry/michelle-obama-natural -curls_n_5d235171e4b0f31256879d95.

9. Terresa Moses, "Project Naptural: A Socio-Cultural Initiative for Naptural Living" (MA thesis, Univ. of North Texas, 2015).

10. *Transition* is the process of growing out Black hair while keeping its chemically relaxed ends until a desired length is reached. Once this occurs, the chemically processed or heat-damaged parts are cut off. Blending the two textures of hair as one tries to retain length may become difficult.

    Big chop refers to the haircut that removes all chemically treated parts of hair. After the big chop, someone is left with a very short length of hair often referred to as a *TWA* (teeny weeny Afro).

11. Taylor Gee, "Something Is Rotten in the State of Minnesota," *Politico Magazine,* July 16, 2016, https://www.politico.com/magazine/story/2016/07/minnesota-race -inequality-philando-castile-214053.

12. The word *Beady-beads* describes the naps or coils on the edge of the hairline. These are most prominent if a woman processes her hair with a chemical relaxer and pulls her hair up to reveal new growth that has not been processed and thus has a curly texture.

    Kitchen refers to the edges on the back of the head of hair, near the neck, that are the hardest to keep straight. See the photos in Christina J., "7 Ways You Should Care for Your Nape Hair," *Black Hair Information.com,* Apr. 8, 2021, blackhairinformation.com/general-articles/tips/7-ways-care-nape-hair/.

    Tender-headed describes Black people who endure much pain while their hair is manipulated, that is, combed, straightened, or otherwise aggressively styled.

13. "Hair Products for Natural and Black Hair," *Andre Walker Hair,* accessed July 19, 2019 (article unavailable Sept. 22, 2022), https://andrewalkerhair.com/.

14. "There's Hidden Danger in Black Hair Products." *Houston Fibroids,* Dec. 23, 2020, https://houstonfibroids.com/posts/fibroid-symptoms/warning-your-hair -products-could-be-hurting-you/.

15. Cheryl Thompson, "Black Women, Beauty, and Hair as a Matter of Being," *Women's Studies* 38, no. 8 (2009): 831–56.

16. *Good Hair,* directed by Jeff Stilson (New York: HBO Films, 2009), DVD.

17. Maggie O'Neill, "Transnational Refugees: The Transformative Role of Art?," *Forum: Qualitative Social Research* 9, no. 2 (2008), http://nbn-resolving.de/urn:nbn :de:0114-fqs0802590.

18. Dana Oliver, "These Are Bantu Knots, Not 'Mini Buns.' There's a Difference," *HuffPost,* May 28, 2015, https://www.huffpost.com/entry/bantu-knots-mini -buns-difference_n_7452532#:~:text='%20There's%20A%20Difference.,-By& text=It's%20been%20well%20over%20a,Marc%20by%20Marc%20Jacobs%20 show.&text=Bantu%20knots%20are%20said%20to,Zulu%20tribes%20in%20 southern%20Africa.

About the Contributors

DR. TAMEKA N. ELLINGTON is a fashion scholar; educator; motivational speaker; and expert on diversity, equity, and inclusion initiatives. She began her journey as a researcher on Black dress and hair in 2002. She published several academic journal articles and encyclopedia entries on Black hair during her academic career at Kent State University. She is the cocurator of the Kent State University Museum's internationally acclaimed, award-winning exhibition *TEXTURES: the history and art of Black hair* and its accompanying catalog featuring more than 150 artifacts and contemporary works.

DR. MIKAILA BROWN has a PhD in anthropology and education from Columbia University. Her work centers around the intersections of fashion, race, and equity, with much of her research focusing on issues of inequity endemic to the fashion business ecosystem. After running fashion-related businesses for eleven years, she began teaching fashion business management and DEI (diversity, equity, and inclusion) courses for Cornell University. She is now associate director of Inclusion, Equity, and Inclusion Programming for eCornell, the university's online continuing education arm. She also offers DEI consulting, coaching, and educational trainings to companies like MasterCard, Guess, and Children's Aid, and she leads diversity trainings for many universities, including the Fashion Institute of Technology and John Jay.

DR. LAUREN CROSS is assistant professor of interdisciplinary art and design studies at the University of North Texas. Her research addresses interdisciplinary topics within the visual arts and design, including critical race theory, visual culture, multicultural women's and gender studies. She is an artist, curator, and scholar who holds an MFA in visual arts from Lesley University in Cambridge,

Massachusetts, and a PhD in multicultural women's and gender studies from Texas Woman's University in Denton, Texas.

DR. ANNETTE LYNCH is a professor in the Textiles and Apparel Program at the University of Northern Iowa and the cofounder of the Center for Violence Prevention on her campus. She is the coeditor of *Ethnic Dress in the United States: A Cultural Encyclopedia* (2015). Her research also focuses on the role of dress and appearance in negotiating gender-role transformation and cultural change, particularly within the United States. Her book, *Dress, Gender and Cultural Change: Asian American and African American Rites of Passage* (1999) examines the role that dress worn in rites of passage has in modifying and reinventing tradition and gender ideals for Hmong and African American teenagers and young adults.

DR. AFIYA MBILISHAKA is a clinical psychologist, hairstylist, and hair historian who uses hair as an entry point into mental health care. She is an alumna of the University of Pennsylvania and Howard University. She is the founder of PsychoHairapy LLC and Ma'at Psychological Services.

DR. TALÉ A. MITCHELL is associate professor of advertising at James Madison University. She holds a PhD in media communications and advertising strategy from the University of Illinois Institute of Communication Research, Champaign-Urbana, an MS in advertising, and a BFA in visual communications. Her research explores the intersections among consumer behavior, marketing strategies, and traditional and digital media influence. She also investigates branded entertainment related to consumer behavior, persuasion, effectiveness, emotions, and race. Talé is the director of the JMU in LA Study Away program and currently teaches social media advertising and advertising campaigns. Her professional experience is in marketing, advertising, and graphic design.

TERRESA MOSES (she/her) is a proud Black queer woman dedicated to the liberation of Black and brown people through art and design. She is the creative director at Blackbird Revolt and assistant professor of graphic design and the director of design justice at the University of Minnesota. As a community-engaged scholar, she created Project Naptural and cocreated Racism Untaught. She is currently a PhD candidate in social justice education at the University of Toronto. She serves as a core team member of African American Graphic Designers and as a collaborator with the Black Liberation Lab.

DR. TAURA TAYLOR is assistant professor of sociology at Morehouse College in Atlanta, Georgia. Her research centers intersectionality, agency, and everyday resistance. Her publications include several articles and book chapters, and her current project includes a book proposal based on her dissertation, "Hair That Moves: Black Solidarity, Cognitive Pluralism, and the Natural Hair Social Movement."

LADOSHA WRIGHT has combined her career as an outreach worker and sa-lon owner to style, write about, and advocate for hair. As an activist, she helped modify Ohio's educational standards in cosmetology and barbering. She's a certified master colorist, educator, and public speaker. She is the author of *Curly Hair Adventures* (2016) and *What They Don't Tell You at the Hair Salon* (2018). She traveled to Brusubi, in the Gambia, to write that nation's first-ever cosmetology curriculum and opened the Wright Library.

Index

Page references in italics refer to illustrations.

Black hair. *See* hair, Black

Black is Beautiful movement, 6, 86

Black Lives Matter (BLM) movement, 84, 87–88, 90, 92, 93

Black Nationalists, 86

Black-Owned Beauty Supply Association, 4

Black Panthers/Black Panther Party, 6, 10, 11, 31, 32, 85

Black Power movement, 7–8, 84–85, 87, 92–93

Black Pride movement, 30–31, 32

Black self-hatred theory, 5

Black women: activism of, 85–87, 92–93; bodies of, 101, 108; celebration of, 84; conceptualization by, 113; cultural trauma of, 107; discrimination of, 88–89; empowerment of, 92; within entertainment industry, 89; epistemic authority of, 113; hair preferences of, 100–101; hair requirements of, 28; hair significance to, 133; hairstyle visibility of, 103–4; health compromises of, 106; lack of support for, 74; within media, 42, 90–91; mothering practices of, 109–10; negative feelings of, 71; social cognitive reasoning strategies of, 112; social pressure of, 88, 89; society's treatment of, 59; stereotypes of, 4; technological presence of, 117–28

"the blanket" (Woodson), 25–26

blogging, 125, 126

Bottner, Irving, 3

boycott, of hair products, 4

Brathwaite, Kwame, 87

Bronfenbrenner, Urie, 131–32

Brooks, Wanda, 40, 51

Brown, Elaine, 92

brown girl dreaming (Woodson): "deep in my heart, i do believe" part within, 30–31; "followed the sky's mirrored constellation to freedom" within, 29–30; "i am born" part within, 23–24; overview of, 21–23, 33–34; "ready to change the world" part within, 32–33; "the stories of south carolina run like rivers" part within, 24–29

Brown White, Shauntae, 121

Bubble Guppies, 48

burning hair, semiotics of, 26

Byrd, Ayana, 39, 100

Cannolene Company, *9*

capitalism, 93–95

Carlos, John, 87

Carmichael, Stokely, 85

Carol's Daughter, 94

Catastrophe Management Solutions (CMS), 63

"changes" (Woodson), 26–27

chemicals: damage from, 75, 78, 139; opposition to, 58, 99, 109; overview of, 105, 139. *See also* perm/permed hair; relaxed hair/relaxers; straightened hair

Cherry, Matthew A., 48

children, hair future of, 109–10

children's media, 41, 46–47

Civil Rights Act, 61, 63, 89

civil rights movement, 7–8, 28–29

Clarke, Juanne, 10

clothing, advertisements for, 13–14

colorism, 4–5, 40

communication, variables regarding, 5

confessional poetry, 21–22

confusion phase of Black history, 140

conk, 16

Cooks, Carlos A., 87

cornrows, 48, 55, 64, 89, 102, 136, 141, *148*

counter-frames, 102

Craig, Maxine Leeds, 100

creamy crack, 105

Creating a Respectable and Open World for Naturals (CROWN) Act (California), 64, 74, 78–79, 89

Crenshaw, Kimberlé, 132

criminal theme, 63–64

critical race theory (CRT), 43–44

Cullors, Patrisse, 92

cultural appropriation, 142–43

cultural trauma, 107

Cuomo, Andrew, 64

Cuomo, Mario, 89

Curly Hair Adventures (Wright), 47–48, 49

CurlyNikki.com, 122, 124

cyberella, theory of, 117–18. *See also* Afro-cyberellas

Davis, Angela, 32

Davis, Viola, 90

"deep in my heart, i do believe" (Woodson), 30–31

de León, Aya, 49

diaspora, 31, 94–95

didactic hair culture, 103

digital platforms, Black hair information on, 118–19, 124–25, 127–28. *See also* social media; *and specific platforms*

digital storytelling, 126–27

Dignity for All Students Act (New York), 64

discrimination, 34, 61, 134, 142

disillusion phase of Black history, 140

Disney, 41–42

diversity, within Black hair politics, 92–93

Doc McStuffins, 48

Donahoo, Saran, 100

dreadlocks: changes regarding, 64–65; criminal and humiliating theme regarding, 63–64; culture and ancestry regarding, 58–59; defined, 55; history of, 55–57; microaggressions and, 62; perceptions of self regarding, 59–60; personal stories regarding, 58–59; process of creating, 58; professionalism and, 60–61; racial profiling and, 61; rebellion and, 59; social media and, 62–63; social pressure regarding, 61–62; stand your ground theme regarding, 63; stigmas regarding, 57–58

Du Bois, W. E. B., 85

House, Tyler, 61–62
house negro, 40
Howard, Krystal, 21
Hughes, Clair, 22
humiliating theme, 63–64
Huyer, Sophia, 117

identity, 24, 25, 69
"I Love My Hair" (*Sesame Street*), 46–47, 48–49
inclusion, within Black hair politics, 92–93
infants, 39
Instagram, 118, 119, 123, 125, 127
interactive designs, for website experience, 126
intersectionality, 132
isolation phase of Black history, 140

Jackson, Jesse, 4
Jacobs, Marc, 142–43
Jacobs-Huey, Lanita, 100
Jamaicans, 56
Jheri curl, 10, 13
Johnson, Alexis McGill, 88, 100
Johnson, Andrew, 63–64
Johnson, George, 93
Johnson Products, 93
Jones, Alice, 42
Jones, Chastity, 63, 88–89
journey, natural hair, 73, 131–33

Kaepernick, Colin, 90
Kardashian, Kim, 14
Khalifa, Wiz, 57
King, Martin Luther, Jr., 85
King, Vanessa, 90
kinky hair, 10
Kisob, Princess, 149
Knowles, Solange, 90
Koreans, 7, 94
Kravitz, Lenny, 57

Lancour, NaTasha, 149
Lathan, Sanaa, 75
Lauper, Cyndi, 14
law enforcement, targeting by, 87
Lee, Latoya, 118
Léon, Aya de. *See* de Léon, Aya
Levine, Robert N., 106
Life Studies (Lowell), 21–22
Lil Wayne, 57
The Little Mermaid, 42
Little Rascals, 74
locs. *See* dreadlocks
l'Oréal, 94
Lowell, Robert, 21
Lucid LivingTV, 124
Lynch, Marshawn, 57

MacFarlane, Jessica, 88
Madonna, 14
Malcolm X, 85
Malone, Annie, 3, 26, 93, 94
Maloney, Alan, 63–64
mannequins, hairstyling on, *141, 142, 148*
Marcus Cinema, 61–62
marketing, 127
Marley, Bob, 56
Martin, Trayvon, 84
Mastro, Dana, 4
Mbilishaka, Afiya, 74
McGriff, Natalie, 45, 47
McLarren, Jara, *147, 148*
McNair, Jonda C., 40, 51
media: African Americans within, 4–5; Afro-textured hair celebration within, 46–47; critical race theory (CRT) and, 43–44; negative messages within, 49–50; politics of Black hair within, 90–92; self-acceptance encouragement within, 47–48; self-love acceptance within, 47–48; study sample from, 44–45; white standard of beauty within children's media, 41–42. *See also* social media; *and specific shows/movies*
#melaninpoppin, 125
memoirs, 21
Mercer, Kobena, 100
microaggressions, 43, 62
Milady curriculum, 112
military, grooming codes within, 100
Miró, Estaban Rodriguez, 107–8
Mitchell, Holly, 89
Mizani, 15
models, within advertising, 13–14
Moore, Alix, 11
Morrison, Toni, 57
MOVE, 57
My Nappy Roots, 88
Mystery Black, 9

Nappily Ever After, 75
Nappturality.com, 119, 122, 124, 125–26
nappy hair: negative connotation regarding, 74, 76, 142; within slavery, 139; writings regarding, 34, 46, 48, 88. *See also* naptural hair
Nappy Hair (Herron), 34
Naptura185, 122, 127
naptural hair, 131, 132, 134–35
natural hair, Black: bias against, 89; celebration of, 100; defined, 70; education regarding, 106–7, 119, 122; family and friends as unsupportive regarding, 73–75, 104; fear regarding, 76; health regarding, 77; inclusivity and, 93; journey regarding, 73, 131–33; learning to love, 106–9; learning to reject, 104–6; limitations regarding, 74; media politics regarding, 90–92; negative experiences regarding, 72–73;

negative self-perceptions regarding, 132; "The Perceptions of African Americans on their Natural Hair" questionnaire regarding, 75–76; products for, 94; professionalism and, 88; public perceptions regarding, 88, 135; quality of life regarding, 76–78; reconceptualization of, 108, 112; scoldings regarding, 105; self-esteem/self-schema regarding, 75–76, 78; as spiritual journey, 77; statistics regarding, 71–72, 77; stereotypes regarding, 74–75; trendiness of, 111; unity through, 95; vocabulary for, 106–7. *See also* hair, Black

Natural Hair Does Care, 124

natural hair movement: within digital platforms, 118–19; feminist and womanist frameworks within, 119–20; history of, 56–57; media influence on, 44–45; overview of, 11, 87–88, 100–101; parties within, 100–101; significance of, 95; on social media, 119–21, 122

Newsom, Gavin, 64

Newton, Huey, 85

New York State Human Rights Law (NYSHRL), 64, 74, 89

Niabaly, Dieynaba, 90

Nixon, Angie, 45

North, hairstyle requirements within the, 28

Obama, Michelle, 133

Olajide, Tina, 48

Oliver, Denise, 92

O'Neill, Maggie, 140

Onyejiaka, Tiffany, 5, 10

Opie, Tina, 149

oppression, 102

"our father, fading away" (Woodson), 30

Oyinloye, Sandra, 137, 148

pamoja, 8, 15

Pantene, 16

Parker, Tiana, 61, 89

"The Perceptions of African Americans on their Natural Hair" questionnaire, 75–76

perm/permed hair, 70, 77, 105

physical characteristics, of African Americans, 6

pickaninny, 74

Pierce, Chester, 42–43

Plath, Sylvia, 21

Players, 14

poetry, 21–22. *See also specific poems*

politics, of Black hair: in the 1960s and 1970s, 84–87; capitalism's effects on, 93–95; current, 87–88; diversity and inclusion within, 92–93; within the media, 90–92; overview of, 119–20; in workplace, 88–89

"The Politics of Black Women's Hair" study, 90

pony hawk, 136

"power to the people" (Woodson), 32–33

pressed hair, 70, 77, 105. *See also* straightened hair

The Princess and the Frog (movie), 42

products, hair: African American–owned company characteristics regarding, 6, 13, 14, 15; boycott of, 4; function of, 4; ingredients for, 3; monetary value of industry of, 93–94; ownership statistics regarding, 6, 7; symposium for, 149, 150; workshop regarding, 144

professionalism, 60–61, 88–89, 100

Project Naptural: financial support for, 137; hair-itage poster series and exhibition within, 135–37, 146; implications regarding, 150–51; overview of, 133–34; research methods regarding, 134–35; 2018 symposium of, 145–50, 147, 150; 2018 workshops of, 137–45; workbooks of, 138

Pro-Line, 14

Pro-Line's Curly Kit, 13

Proud Lady icon (AHBAI), 3

Puffy (de Léon), 49

racial profiling, 61

racism, 43, 101

Ramp, James, 57

Raschka, Chris, 46, 48

Rastas, 56–57

"ready to change the world" (Woodson), 32–33

rebellion, 59

refugees, emotional experience of, 140–41

relaxed hair/relaxers: defined, 70; effects of, 139; harmful effects of, 88; personal story regarding, 109–10; process of, 105–6; as restrictive, 77

Revlon, 6

"ribbons" (Woodson), 27–28

Rock, Chris, 59, 105, 139

Rooks, Noliwe, 100

Royal Shield, 8, 9

safe space, 124–25, 127–28

Sakabo, Rachel, 62

Saturday night hair preparation, 26

"say it loud" (Woodson), 32

Selassie, Haile, 56

self-acceptance, 47–48

self-esteem, 69–70, 75–76, 78

self-love, 47–48

self-portraits, 143, 144

self-schema, 75–76

semiotics, 4

Sesame Street, 42–43, 46–47, 48–49, 51

Sexton, Anne, 21

sexuality, clothing and, 13–14

Shakur, Assata, 92

Shea Moisture, 8–9

sisterlock, 58

skin bleaching creams, 9–10

skin color/tone, 6, 9–10, 40

slavery, 28, 40, 43, 55–56